WISE QUOTES

Over 2,000 Positive and Thought Inspiring Short Quotes!

Collected by Steven Hunter

Text copyright © 2015 Steven L. Hunter

All Rights Reserved

Preface

I started collecting quotes by accident. I had a small whiteboard outside my office for messages. One day, I wrote a quote that I thought was profound. A week later, I changed the whiteboard to another quote that I also liked.

A short while later, someone stopped by and said "I like what you are doing putting these quotes on your whiteboard." I never intended to continue updating the quotes, but it sounded like an interesting challenge to keep coming up with quotes.

I read through a book of quotes that I had and pulled out ones that were positive or thought provoking. The quotes also had to be short enough to fit on a small message whiteboard.

The quote book got me started, but I continued looking for other quotes. Once you start looking for anything, you are likely to see it everywhere. It also occurred to me to check out some of the quote websites. Soon, I had enough quotes that I went from updating the whiteboard once a day instead of once a week.

My office has moved several times over the years, but I kept putting up quotes, even if I had to get a new whiteboard for my new office. Hardly a week goes by without someone saying how much they enjoy my quotes. That is why I do it. It is my gift to my coworkers.

I figured that I should share outside of my workplace also, so I started the Twitter® account "@StevesQuotes". Since the quotes are short enough to fit on a small whiteboard, they fit on a Twitter® message.

These quotes encompass the wisdom of many hundreds of people both alive and long dead. We are all indebted to their words of wisdom.I hope that you enjoy and share these quotes.

Table of Contents

(by author's last name)

A	5
B	14
C	27
D	37
E	44
F	51
G	57
H	62
I	72
J	73
K	77
L	83
M	91
N	102
O	105
P	108
Q	117
R	118
S	127
T	136
V	142
W	144
Y	150
Z	151

A

One man can be a crucial ingredient on a team, but one man cannot make a team
Kareem Abdul-Jabbar

By doubting we come to the question, and by seeking we may come upon the truth
Pierre Abelard

Innovation cannot be decoupled from creative destruction
Daron Acemoglu

The sun will shine on those who stand before it
Chinua Achebe 5-15-20

If you don't like someone's story, write your own
Chinua Achebe

One of the truest tests of integrity is its blunt refusal to be compromised
Chinua Achebe

Nobody can teach me who I am
Chinua Achebe

Great necessities call out great virtues
Abigail Adams

Learning is not attained by chance; it must be sought...with ardor and diligence
Abigail Adams

There is nothing worse than a sharp image of a fuzzy subject
Ansel Adams

I have found that every experience is a form of exploration
Ansel Adams

A teacher affects eternity; he can never tell where his influence stops
Henry Adams

Old minds are like old horses; you must exercise them if you wish to keep them in working order
John Adams

If your actions inspire others to dream more, learn more, do more and become more, you are a leader
John Quincy Adams

There is no such thing as a small act of kindness
Scott Adams

The best things in life are silly
Scott Adams

If I didn't mold my reality, then I'd still be in the ghetto
William Adams

Cheerfulness keeps up a kind of daylight in the mind
Joseph Addison

What sculpture is to a block of marble, education is to an human soul
Joseph Addison

A thick skin is a gift from God
Konrad Adenauer

It is easier to fight for one's principles than live up to them
Alfred Adler

No act of kindness, no matter how small, is ever wasted
Aesop

It is easy to be brave from a distance
Aesop

We hang the petty thieves and appoint the great ones to public office
Aesop

Better to be wise by the misfortunes of others than by your own
Aesop

If it worked wrong once and you didn't fix it, it ain't fixed
David Agans

If you don't practice, you don't deserve to win
Andre Agassi

Miracles can be made, but only by sweating
Giovanni Agnelli

You can tell more about a person by what he says about others than you can by what others say about him
Leo Aikman

Excuses are merely nails used to build a house of failure
HabeebAkande

A positive attitude may not solve all your problems, but it will annoy enough people to make it worth the effort
    Herm Albright

Concentrate, play your game and don't be afraid to win
    Amy Alcott

Many argue; not many converse
    Luisa May Alcott

You have to leave the city of your comfort and go into the wilderness of your intuition
    Alan Alda

It is always better to be wise than to be smart
    Alan Alda

Be brave enough to live life creatively
    Alan Alda

To achieve more and better results, more resourcefulness is as important as more resources
    Tony Alessandra

Do unto others as they would have you do unto them
    Tony Alessandra

Good enough, isn't
    Tony Alessandra

Time heals all wounds, unless you pick at them
    Shaun Alexander

Adversity is wisdom's testing ground
    Henry Alford

The man who has no imagination has no wings
    Muhammad Ali

It isn't the mountains ahead to climb that wear you out; it's the pebble in your shoe.
    Muhammad Ali

Service to others is the rent you pay for your room here on earth
    Muhammad Ali

Wars against nations are fought to change maps; wars against poverty are fought to map change
    Muhammad Ali

I had it in my heart. I believed in myself
Muhammad Ali

Success is not achieved by winning all the time
Muhammad Ali

No one starts out on top
Muhammad Ali

It's lack of faith that makes people afraid of meeting challenges
Muhammad Ali

Your ability to generate power is directly proportional to your ability to relax
David Allen

Go for direction, not perfection
David Allen

Clear the deck, create a context, and do some creative project thinking.
David Allen

We can be quietly active and actively quiet
David Allen

There's an inverse relationship between the amount something is on your mind and how much it's getting done
David Allen

If there's something bothering you, chances are that you are the bottleneck
David Allen

Your mind is a great place to have ideas, but a terrible place to manage them
David Allen

What we truly need to do is often what we most feel like avoiding
David Allen

The best way to have a good idea is to have as many bad ones as you can
David Allen

People with many interests live, not only longest, but happiest
George Allen

Winning can be defined as the science of being totally prepared
George Allen

Circumstances do not make the man, they reveal him
    JamesAllen

The more tranquil a man becomes, the greater his success
    James Allen

Life is like an analogy
    Aaron Allston

A strong sense of self is our base of operations for everything we do in life
    Julia Alvarez

No duty is more urgent than that of returning thanks
    St.Ambrose

All appears to change when we change
    Henri-Frederic Amiel

Prayer begins where human capacity ends
    Marian Anderson

Fear is a disease that eats away at logic
    Marian Anderson

People who live in the past generally are afraid to compete in the present
    Sparkey Anderson

The first and most difficult risk that we can take is to be honest with ourselves
    Walter Anderson

If everything seems under control, you're just not going fast enough
    Mario Andretti

If you wait, all that happens is that you get older
    Mario Andretti

Perseverance is failing 19 times and succeeding the 20th
    Julie Andrews

What I spent, is gone; what I kept, I lost; but what I gave away will be mine forever
    Ethel Andrus

Success is liking yourself, liking what you do, and liking how you do it
    Maya Angelou

A bird doesn't sing because it has an answer, it sings because it has a song
    Maya Angelou

Bitterness is like cancer. It eats its host.
    Maya Angelou

We may encounter many defeats, but we must not be defeated
    MayaAngelou

All great achievements require time
    MayaAngelou

If you don't stay moving, they will throw dirt on you
    Paul Anka

Accomplish something every day of your life
    Walter Annenberg

A person who aims at nothing is sure to hit it
    Anonymous

Experience is a good teacher, but she sends in terrific bills
    Minna Antrim

To one who has faith, no explanation is necessary. To one without faith, no explanation is possible.
    Thomas Aquinas

I would rather die a meaningful death than live meaningless life
    Corazon Aquino

My favorite thing is to go where I've never been
    Diane Arbus

An executive is only as good as his health
    Jeffrey Archer

In order to go on living, one must try to escape the death involved in perfectionism
    Hannah Arendt

By words the mind is winged
    Aristophanes

It is the mark of an educated mind to be able to entertain a thought without accepting it
    Aristotle

We are what we repeatedly do
> *Aristotle*

We make war that we may live in peace
> *Aristotle*

The whole is more than the sum of its parts
> *Aristotle*

A friend is a second self
> *Aristotle*

Education is the best provision for the journey to old age
> *Aristotle*

Happiness depends upon ourselves
> *Aristotle*

Pleasure in the job puts perfection in the work
> *Aristotle*

The fate of empires depends on the education of youth
> *Aristotle*

The educated differ from the uneducated as much as the living from the dead
> *Aristotle*

The worst form of inequality is to try to make unequal things equal
> *Aristotle*

Quality is not an act. It is a habit.
> *Aristotle*

Moral excellence comes about as a result of habit
> *Aristotle*

If you ever get a second chance in life for something, you've got to go all the way
> *Lance Armstrong*

Honesty is the cornerstone of all success
> *Mary Kay Ash*

You can go as far as your mind lets you
> *Mary Kay Ash*

A good goal is like a strenuous exercise - it makes you stretch
> *Mary Kay Ash*

Unless you try something beyond what you've already mastered, you will never grow
> *Vicki Ash*

It's not what you know that makes you better, it's what you're willing to learn
> *Vicki Ash*

Sandwich every bit of criticism between two layers of praise
> *Mary Kay Ask*

It takes time to get a dance right, to create something memorable
> *Fred Astaire*

Power is the ability to do good things for others
> *Brooke Astor*

Science is the only true guide in life
> *Mustafa Atatürk*

Love is a gift and cannot be earned. It can only be given.
> *Gordon Atkinson*

If you don't run your own life, somebody else will
> *John Atkinson*

Step by step, and the thing is done
> *Charles Atlas*

Music washes away from the soul the dust of everyday life
> *Berthold Auerbach*

When was the last time you heard someone criticized for listening too much?
> *Norm Augustine*

Very little is needed to make a happy life
> *Marcus Aurelius*

The art of living is more like wrestling than dancing
> *Marcus Aurelius*

If a thing is humanly possible, consider it to be within your reach
> *Marcus Aurelius*

Our life is what our thoughts make it
> *Marcus Aurelius*

No man pleases by silence; many please by speaking briefly
> *Decimus Ausonius*

B

The haven of peace is in yourself
    Satya Sai Baba

Let him who would enjoy a good future waste none of his present
    Roger Babson

The successful man is the one who had the chance and took it
    Roger Babson

What the caterpillar calls the end of the world, the Master calls a butterfly
    Richard Bach

Ask yourself the secret of your success. Listen to your answer, and practice it.
    Richard Bach

The mold of a man's fortune is in his own hands
    Francis Bacon

A wise man will make more opportunities than he finds
    FrancisBacon

We judge a man by how he honors his responsibilities
    Robert Baden-Powell

We never fail when we try to do our duty, we always fail when we neglect to do it
    Robert Baden-Powell

The greatest pleasure in life is doing what people say you cannot do
    Walter Bagehot

He who graduates today, and stops learning tomorrow, is uneducated the day after
    Newton Baker

It doesn't pay to get discouraged
    Lucile Ball

The more things you do, the more you can do
    Lucile Ball

The best energy bar is the barbell
    Craig Ballantyne

The older I get, the more I try not to waste my time on negative energy
    Christine Baranski

I learned long ago to accept the fact that not everything I create will see the light of day
    Joseph Barbera

It is always the simple that produces the marvelous
    Amelia Barr

Work is either fun or drudgery. It depends on your attitude. I like fun.
    Colleen Barrett

Those who bring sunshine into the lives of others cannot keep it from themselves   7-6-20
    James Barrie

Always be a little kinder than necessary   2-25
    James Barrie

The best time to make friends is before you need them
    Ethel Barrymore

You grow up the day you have your first real laugh - at yourself
    Ethel Barrymore

A man is not old until regrets take the place of dreams
    John Barrymore

When everyone gets on the same side of the boat, the result is inevitable
    D.R. Barton

The art of living lies less in eliminating our troubles than is growing with them
    Bernard Baruch

You don't have to blow out the other fellow's light to let your own shine
    Bernard Baruch

Patience is never more important than when you are at the edge of losing it   3-16
    O.A. Battista

The best inheritance a parent can give his children is a few minutes of his time each day
    Orlando Battista

Initiative is to success what a lighted match is to a candle
    Orlando Battista

Sometimes you have to reach great heights to realize how small you are
    Felix Baumgartner

There should be no distinction between fine art and applied industrial design
    Herbert Bayer

Change your life today. Don't gamble on the future
    Simone de Beauvoir

It's not a very big step from contentment to complacency
    Simone de Beauvoir

No man can tell whether he is rich or poor by turning to his ledger
    Henry Beecher

In this world it is not what we take up, but what we give up, that makes us rich
    Henry Beecher

The first hour of the morning is the rudder of the day
    Henry Beecher

The first hour is the rudder of the day
    Henry Beecher

Positive things happen to positive people
    Sarah Beeny

A man is what he makes of himself
    Alexander Bell

There are no menial jobs, only menial attitudes
    William Bennett

Happiness is like a cat, if you try to coax it or call it, it will avoid you
    William Bennett

Trust is the lubrication that makes it possible for organizations to work
    Warren Bennis

Pride is concerned with who is right. Humility is concerned with what is right
    Ezra Benson

Think like a man of action, and act like a man of thought
  HenriBergson

If opportunity doesn't knock, build a door
  Milton Berle

Laughter is an instant vacation 2-14
  Milton Berle

Life is 10% what you make it and 90% how you take it
  Irving Berlin

Talent is only a starting point
  Irving Berlin

Time is the best teacher. Unfortunately, it kills all its pupils
  Hector-Louis Berlioz

It is what we think we know already that often prevents us from learning
  Claude Bernard

Art is I; science is we
  ClaudeBernard

Power does not corrupt men; fools...corrupt power
  GeorgeBernard Shaw

When you come to a fork in the road, take it
  Yogi Berra

If you don't know where you are going, you'll end up someplace else
  Yogi Berra

You can observe a lot just by watching
  Yogi Berra

It ain't over 'til it's over
  Yogi Berra

Ignorance is an evil weed, which dictators may cultivate
  William Beveridge

You earn your reputation by trying to hard things well
  Jeff Bezos

Be like a postage stamp. Stick to one thing until you get there.
  Josh Billings

An optimist is the personification of spring
    Susan Bissonette

You will never find time for anything. If you want time, you must make it.
    Charles Bixton

Winning doesn't always mean being first
    Bonnie Blair

All sorrows can be borne if you can put them into a story
    Karen Blixen

A real friend who comes to the house is a heavenly messenger
    Karen Blixen

We must leave our mark on life while we have it in our power
    Karen Blixen

Friends come and go but enemies accumulate
    Arthur Bloch

No matter how good an idea sounds, test it first
    Henry Bloch

School is never out for the professional
    Bob Bly

Perfect does not mean perfect actions in a perfect world, but appropriate actions in an imperfect one
    R. H. Blythe

It's an all-too-human frailty to suppose that a favorable wind will blow forever
    Rick Bode

Creativity is thinking of new things. Innovation does them.
    Lisa Bodell

When we hold back on life, life holds us back
    Mary Boggs

A positive attitude causes a chain reaction of positive thoughts
    Wade Boggs

An expert is a man who has made all the mistakes which can be made, in a narrow field
    Niels Bohr

Prediction is very difficult, especially if it's about the future
Niels Bohr

There are some things so serious you have to laugh at them
Niels Bohr

How often the fear of one evil leads us to a worse
Nicolas Boileau-Despreaux

Honor is like a rugged island without a shore; once you have left it, you cannot return
Nicholas Boileau

You can't assume there is a lot of time to do what you like
Marc Bolan

It takes a lot of courage to show your dreams to someone else
Erma Bombeck

Imagination rules the world
Napoleon Bonaparte

He who fears being conquered is sure of defeat
Napoleon Bonaparte

A leader is a dealer in hope
Napoleon Bonaparte

Courage is going on when you don't have the strength to go on
Napoleon Bonaparte

Action springs not from thought, but from a readiness for responsibility
Dietrich Bonhoeffer

It is only possible to live happily-ever-after on a day-to-day basis
Margaret Bonnano 8-18-20

The greatest obstacle to discovery is not ignorance - it is the illusion of knowledge
Daniel Boorstin

If you desire peace, cultivate justice
Norman Borlaug

Losing an illusion makes you wiser than finding a truth
Ludwig Börne

At the end of the day, you bet on people, not on strategies
Larry Bossidy

Life is denied by lack of attention, whether it be to cleaning windows or trying to write a masterpiece
    Nadia Boulanger

All models are wrong but some are useful
    George Box

The most important trip you may take in life is meeting people halfway
    Henry Boye

First you jump off the cliff and you build wings on the way down
    Ray Bradbury

If computers get too powerful, we can organize them into a committee — that will do them in
    Bradley

The first step toward change is awareness. The second step is acceptance
    Nathaniel Branden

In a creative business with an emphasis on experiment and development, ideas are the lifeblood
    Richard Branson

Business opportunities are like buses. There's always another one coming.
    Richard Branson

Life is like sailing.You can use any wind to go in any direction.
    Robert Brault

Where the loser saw barriers, the winner saw hurdles
    Robert Brault

It's never too late to have a happy childhood.
    Berke Breathed

Striving and struggle precede success, even in the dictionary
    Sarah Breathnach

Life isn't fair, but it's still good
    Regina Brett

When in doubt, just take the next small step
    Regina Brett

Life is too short to waste time hating anyone
    Regina Brett

Make peace with your past so it won't screw up the present
Regina Brett

Take a deep breath. It calms the mind.
Regina Brett

Over prepare, then go with the flow
Regina Brett

No one is in charge of your happiness but you
Regina Brett

What other people think of you is none of your business
Regina Brett

However good or bad a situation is, it will change
Regina Brett

Don't take yourself so seriously. No one else does.
Regina Brett

Growing old beats the alternative -- dying young
Regina Brett

Your children get only one childhood
Regina Brett

Life isn't tied with a bow, but it's still a gift
Regina Brett

All of life's great lessons present themselves again and again until mastered
David Brewer

One of the greatest feelings in the world is knowing that we as individuals can make a difference
JeffBridges

A successful man is one who can lay a firm foundation with the bricks that others have thrown at him
David Brinkley

How delightful to find a friend in everyone
Joseph Brodsky

Think of your education as your ticket to change the world
Tom Brokaw

A man masters nature not by force, but by understanding
Jacob Bronowski

Do not pray for tasks equal to your powers. Pray for powers equal to your tasks.
> *Phillips Brooks*

Listening, not imitation, may be the sincerest form of flattery
> *Joyce Brothers*

Find ways to relax for at least five minutes every hour and you'll be more productive
> *Joyce Brothers*

A strong, positive self-image is the best possible preparation for success
> *Joyce Brothers*

If you want success, start thinking of yourself as a success
> *Joyce Brothers*

My riches consist not in the extent of my possessions, but in the fewness of my wants
> *Joseph Brotherton*

In the book of life, the answers aren't in the back.
> *Charlie Brown*

Engineers operate at the interface between science and society
> *Dean Brown*

Too many of us are not living our dreams because we are living our fears
> *Les Brown*

Review your goals twice every day in order to be focused on achieving them
> *Les Brown*

You have to know what is right for you and go after it regardless of what others say
> *Les Brown*

Change is difficult but often essential to survival
> *Les Brown*

Help others achieve their dreams and you will achieve yours
> *Les Brown*

You don't get in life what you want, you get in life what you are
> *Les Brown*

Anything worth doing is worth doing poorly, until you learn to do it well
    Steve Brown

Strive for excellence, not perfection
    H. Jackson Brown Jr.

Learn to listen. Opportunity sometimes knocks very softly.
    Jackson Brown Jr.

Think big thoughts but relish small pleasures.
    H. Jackson Brown, Jr.

Nothing is more expensive than a missed opportunity
    H.Jackson Brown, Jr.

Failure is the tuition you pay for success
    WalterBrunell

Destiny is no matter of chance. It is a matter of choice
    William Jennings Bryan

The price of victory is high, but so are the rewards
    Bear Bryant

Show class, have pride, and display character
    Bear Bryant

The fear of being wrong is the prime inhibitor of the creative process
    Jean Bryant

Everything negative is all an opportunity for me
    Kobe Bryant

If you're afraid to fail, then you're probably going to fail
    Kobe Bryant

All journeys have a secret destination of which the traveler is unaware
    Martin Buber

Play is the exultation of the possible
    Martin Buber

Solitude is the place of purification
    Martin Buber

The world is not comprehensible, but it is embraceable
    Martin Buber

To be old can be glorious if one has not unlearned how to begin
Martin Buber

We can pay our debt to the past by putting the future in debt to ourselves
John Buchan

I don't wait for moods. You accomplish nothing if you do that.
Pearl Buck

What we think, we become
Buddha

You will not be punished for your anger, you will be punished by your anger
Buddha

Speak or act with an impure mind and trouble will follow you, as the cart follows the ox
Buddha

Contentment is the greatest wealth
Buddha

You will not be punished for your anger. You will be punished by your anger.
Buddha

Chains of habit are too light to be felt until they are too heavy to be broken
Warren Buffet

If you wait for the robins, spring will be over
Warren Buffett

It is not necessary to do extraordinary things to get extraordinary results
Warren Buffett

It takes 20 years to build a reputation and five minutes to ruin it
Warren Buffett

Risk comes from not knowing what you are doing
Warren Buffett

Pick out associates whose behavior is better than yours, and you'll drift in that direction 8-14-20
Warren Buffett

An honor is not diminished for being shared
  Lois Bujold

The dynamic force of life creates the new over and over again
  Nikolai Bukharin

The tongue can conceal the truth, but the eyes never!
  Mikhail Bulgakov

Let us put our minds together and see what life we can make for our children
  Sitting Bull

What mankind wants is not talent; it is purpose
  Edward Bulwer-Lytton

Talent does what it can, genius does what it must
  Edward Bulwer-Lytton

To read without reflecting is like eating without digesting
  Edmond Burke

Never despair, but if you do, work on in despair
  Edmund Burke

Only I can change my life. No one can do it for me.
  Carol Burnett

I have always grown from my problems and challenges
  Carol Burnett

When you have a dream, you've got to grab it and never let go
  Carol Burnett

No one ever said life was fair. Just Eventful.
  Carol Burnett

Make no little plans; they have no magic to stir men's blood
  Daniel Burnham

Don't miss out on life just to stay alive
  Adam Burrell

A quiet mind cureth all
  Robert Burton

Time has no meaning in itself unless we choose to give it significance
  Leo Buscaglia

A single rose can be my garden
    Leo Buscaglia

If you miss love, you miss life
    Leo Buscaglia

To know and not to do is not to know
    LeoBuscaglia

The most important yardstick of your success will be how you treat other people
    Barbara Bush

Get involved in the big ideas of your time
    Barbara Bush

Cherish your human connections
    Barbara Bush 3-31-22

The ultimate inspiration is the deadline
    Nolan Bushnell

Optimism is the foundation of courage
    Nicholas Butler

Failure is never quite so frightening as regret
    Cliff Buxton

C

A man begins cutting his wisdom teeth the first time he bites off more than he can chew
>*Herb Caen*

Curiosity is the most powerful thing you own
>*James Cameron*

The person that works just for money is a slave
>*Joseph Campbell*

The patriot's blood is the seed of freedom's tree
>*Thomas Campbell*

Real generosity toward the future consists in giving all to what is present
>*Albert Camus*

Life is the sum of all your choices.
>*Albert Camus*

When you're nice to people, they want to be nice back to you
>*Jack Canfield*

People should live full lives and not settle for anything less
>*Jack Canfield*

Failure is the condiment that gives success its flavor
>*Truman Capote*

A hunch is creativity trying to tell you something
>*Frank Capra*

The mystery of the wild is the mystery of creation
>*Philip Caputo*

Narrative is linear, but action has breadth and depth
>*Thomas Carlyle*

The purpose of man is in action not thought
>*Thomas Carlyle*

The man without a purpose is like a ship without a rudder
>*Thomas Carlyle*

The heart always sees before the head can see
>*Thomas Carlyle*

Tell a person they are brave and you help them become so
Thomas Carlyle

The tragedy of life is not so much what men suffer, but rather what they miss
Thomas Carlyle

Not what I have, but what I do is my kingdom
Thomas Carlyle

Silence is more eloquent than words
Thomas Carlyle

Virtue is like health: the harmony of the whole man
Thomas Carlyle

He who has health, has hope; and he who has hope has everything
Thomas Carlyle

Endurance is patience concentrated
Thomas Carlyle

Conviction is worthless unless it is converted into conduct
Thomas Carlyle

Put all your eggs in one basket and watch that basket very carefully
Andrew Carnegie

Indiscriminate charity is one of the most serious obstacles to the improvement of our race
Andrew Carnegie

The easiest thing for a weakling to do is to quit
AndrewCarnegie

Do the hard jobs first. The easy jobs will take care of themselves
Dale Carnegie

To be liked, you have to be the one to reach out first
Dale Carnegie

The person that goes the furthest is the one who is willing to do and dare
Dale Carnegie

We all have possibilities that we don't know about
Dale Carnegie

To be well liked, you have to be the one to reach out first
Dale Carnegie

The key to whatever success I enjoy today is: Don't ask. Do.
Vikki Carr

Happiness is being dissolved into something complete and great
Willa Carther

When you can do the common things in life in an uncommon way, you will command the attention of the world
George Washington Carver

Pain is inevitable. Suffering is optional.
M. Kathleen Casey

There are some things you learn best in calm, and some in storm
Willa Cather

Man's biggest mistake is to believe that he's working for someone else
NashuaCavalier

We live in a rainbow of chaos
Paul Cezanne

It is always so simple, and so complicating, to accept an apology
Michael Chabon

In order to be irreplaceable, one must always be different
Coco Chanel

Success is often achieved by people that don't know that failure is inevitable
Coco Chanel

Don't spend time beating on a wall, hoping to transform it into a door
Coco Chanel

The secret to success is knowing what you don't know
Milton Chang

Arrogance makes you think that you are better than you really are
Milton Chang

They're only truly great who are truly good
GeorgeChapman

I never wanted to be famous. I only wanted to be great.
Ray Charles

Inspiration is the act of drawing up a chair to the writing desk
    Geoffrey Chaucer

Knowledge is of no value unless you put it into practice
    Anton Checkhov

Any idiot can face a crisis - it's day to day living that wears you out.
    Anton Chekhov

Rewards are on the inside
    Kristin Chenoweth

An injury is much sooner forgotten than an insult
    Lord Chesterfield

Don't ever take a fence down until you know the reason it was put up
    G. Chesterson

The true soldier fights not because he hates what is in front of him, but because he loves what is behind him
    G.K. Chesterton

If you wait for the perfect moment when all is safe and assured, it may never arrive
    Maurice Chevalier

Times of advancement are preceded by times of disorder
    I Ching

Success comes to those who can weather the storm
    I Ching

Life is a field of unlimited possibilities
    Deepak Chopra

A beautiful person is someone who stays true to themselves and their spirit
    Helena Christensen

Truth, however bitter, can be woven into a design for living
    Agatha Christie

The real secret to success is enthusiasm
    WalterChrysler

The human body can do so much, and then the heart and spirit take over
    Sung Ki Chung

We make a living by what we get, we make a life by what we give
Winston Churchill

Men occasionally stumble over the truth, but most of them pick themselves up and hurry off as if nothing ever happened
Winston Churchill

A pessimist sees the difficulty in every opportunity; an optimist sees the opportunity in every difficulty
Winston Churchill

Success is not final, failure is not fatal; it is the courage to continue that counts
Winston Churchill

Without courage, all other virtues lose their meaning
Winston Churchill

Democracy is the worst system out there except for all the others
Winston Churchill

I am an optimist. It does not seem too much use being anything else
Winston Churchill

Attitude is a little thing that makes a big difference
Winston Churchill 2-24

To improve is to change; to be perfect is to change often
Winston Churchill

If you're going through hell, keep going
Winston Churchill

Continuous effort is the key to unlocking your potential
Winston Churchill

Meet success like a gentleman; disaster like a man
Winston Churchill

Courage is what it takes to stand up and speak; courage is also what it takes to sit down and listen. 6-26-20
Winston Churchill

The day will happen whether or not you get up
John Ciardi

A room without books is like a body without a soul
Marcus Cicero

If you have a garden and a library, you have everything you need
    Marcus Cicero

The change of fortune test the reliability of friends
    Marcus Cicero

What one has, one ought to use
    Marcus Cicero

If you can find a path with no obstacles, it probably doesn't lead anywhere
    Frank Clark

Life is change. Growth is optional. Choose wisely.
    Karen Clark

Any sufficiently advanced technology is indistinguishable from magic
    Arthur C Clarke

Only feeble minds are paralyzed by facts
    Arthur C. Clarke

The limits of the possible can only be defined by going beyond them
    Arthur C. Clarke

Statistics are no substitute for judgment
    Henry Clay

If you want creative workers, give them enough time to play
    John Cleese

All I know I learned after I was 30
    Georges Clemenceau

In calm water every ship has a good captain
    Grover Cleveland

To live without risk for me would be tantamount to death
    Jacqueline Cochran

In change there is power
    Alan Cohen

When our students fail, we as teachers have failed
    Marva Collins

Hard work has made it easy. That is why I win.
    Nadia Comaneci

If you don't make things happen, then things will happen to you
Lanes Company

Every vital organization owes its birth and life to an exciting and daring idea
James Conant

Forget injuries, never forget kindness
Confucius

To see what is right and not to do it, is want of courage
Confucius

He who learns but does not think, is lost! He who thinks but does not learn is in great danger
Confucius

Men's natures are alike; it is their habits that separate them
Confucius

The more man meditates upon good thoughts, the better will be his world and the world at large
Confucius

He who will not economize will have to agonize
Confucius

Everything has beauty but not everyone sees it
Confucius 9-15-20

Respect yourself and others will respect you.
Confucius

Better a diamond with a flaw than a pebble without
Confucius

Choose a job you love, and you will never have to work a day in your life
Confucius

The strength of a nation derives from the integrity of the home
Confucius

The superior man thinks always of virtue; the common man thinks of comfort
Confucius

He who wishes to secure the good of others has already secured his own
Confucius

He who conquers himself is the mightiest warrior
Confucius

It does not matter how slowly you go so long as you do not stop
Confucius

The mechanic that would perfect his work must first sharpen his tools
Confucius

Thinking is the great enemy of perfection
JosephConrad

A professional is someone who can do his best work when he doesn't feel like it
Alistair Cooke

I have never been hurt by anything I didn't say
Calvin Coolidge

Those who trust to chance must abide by the results of chance
Calvin Coolidge

Don't expect to build up the weak by pulling down the strong
Calvin Coolidge

If you see 10 troubles coming down the road, you can be sure that 9 will run into the ditch before they reach you
Calvin Coolidge

We cannot do everything at once, but we can do something at once
Calvin Coolidge

When you don't know what to do, do the work in front of you
Calvin Coolidge

Danger is the spice of life
Jeff Cooper

Understand the problem. Pull your weight. Appreciate. Be completely honest and trustworthy in all things.
JeffCooper

The reason I exercise is for the quality of life I enjoy
Kenneth Cooper

The same fence that shuts others out shuts you in
William Copeland

In order to succeed, your desire for success should be greater than your fear of failure
>   *Bill Cosby*

I don't know the key to success, but the road to failure is trying to please everybody
>   *Bill Cosby*

Love is a friendship set to music
>   *JosephCossman*

You are younger today than you will ever be again
>   *Norman Cousins*

Wisdom consists of the anticipation of consequences
>   *Norman Cousins*

The patient's hopes are the physician's secret weapon
>   *Norman Cousins*

There are only two lasting bequests we can give our children...one is roots, the other wings
>   *Stephen Covey*

Private victories precede public victories
>   *StephenCovey*

We are free to choose our actions, but we are not free to choose the consequences of these actions
>   *Stephen Covey*

If the automobile had followed the same development cycle as the computer, a Rolls-Royce would today cost $100, get a million miles per gallon, and explode once a year, killing everyone inside.
>   *Robert Cringely*

You can be competitive and still be a good person
>   *Walter Cronkite*

Being convinced one knows the whole story is the surest way to fail
>   *Phil Crosby*

It is better to wear out than to rust out
>   *Richard Cumberland*

It takes courage to grow up and become who you are
>   *E.E. Cummings*

Once we believe in ourselves, we can risk curiosity
>   *E.E. Cummings*

The price of success must be paid in full, and it must be paid in advance. There are no shortcuts.
    John Cummuta

Nothing in life is to be feared. It is only to be understood.
    Marie Curie

The way of progress is neither swift nor easy
    Marie Curie

Nothing straightens your spine like having your back against the wall
    Edith Current

Always plan ahead. It wasn't raining when Noah built the ark.
    Richard Cushing

D

Fear is your friend, if you can control it
Cus D'Amato

Wherever you go, no matter what the weather, always bring your own sunshine.
Anthony D'Angelo

Life is painting a picture, not doing a sum
Sri da Avabhas

Time stays long enough for those who use it
Leonardo Da Vinci

Time stays long enough for anyone who will use it
Leonardo da Vinci

Simplicity is the ultimate sophistication
Leonardo da Vinci

Intelligence without ambition is a bird without wings
Salvador Dali

Who dares to teach must never cease to learn
John Dana

You can only protect your liberties by protecting the other man's freedom
Clarence Darrow

A man's friendships are one of the best measures of his worth
Charles Darwin

A fool is a man who never tried an experiment in his life
Erasmus Darwin

Few people can see genius in someone who has offended them
Robertson Davies

Attempt the impossible in order to improve your work
Bette Davis

This will remain the land of the free only so long as it is the home of the brave
Elmer Davis

Be open-minded, but not so open-minded that our brains drop out
Richard Dawkins

Information's pretty thin stuff unless mixed with experience
Clarence Day

Freedom is the oxygen of the soul
Moshe Dayan

All human power is a compound of time and patience
Honore de Balzac

To be prepared is half the victory
Miguel De Cervantes

Diligence is the mother of good fortune
Miguel de Cervantes

Too much sanity may be madness.
Miguel de Cervantes

The world is round so that friendship may encircle it
Pierre De Chardin

It is not the great temptations that ruin us; it is the little ones
John De Forest

Imagination is the one weapon in the war against reality
Jules de Gaultier

Sometimes being pushed to the wall gives you the momentum necessary to get over it
Peter de Jager

No trumpets sound when the important decisions of our life are made
Agnes de Mille

Even on the most exalted throne in the world we are only sitting on our own bottom
Michael de Montaigne

The most certain sign of wisdom is continual cheerfulness
Michael de Montaigne

We cannot become what we need to be by remaining what we are
Max De Pree

Social order at the expense of liberty is hardly a bargain
Marquis de Sade

Nothing is so strong as gentleness.Nothing is so gentle as real strength.
Frances de Sales

Be who you are and be that well
Francis de Sales

Americans seem to have a genius for collective action
Alexisde Tocqueville

The good thing about science is that it's true whether or not you believe in it
Neil deGrasse Tyson

Creativity is a drug I cannot live without
Cecil DeMille

Learning is not compulsory…neither is survival
Edward Deming

The wrongdoer is more unfortunate than the man wronged
Democritus

Happiness resides not in possessions, and not in gold, happiness dwells in the soul
Democritus

Small opportunities are the beginning of great enterprise
Demosthenes

A champion owes everybody something
Jack Dempsey

It is not enough to have a good mind; the main thing is to use it well
Rene Descartes

Small opportunities are often the beginning of great enterprises
Desmosthenes

If it doesn't challenge you, it doesn't change you
Fred DeVito

Life tends to respond to our outlook, to shape itself to meet our expectations
Richard DeVos

Minds are like parachutes – they only function when open
Thomas Dewar

Education is not preparation for life, education is life itself
John Dewey

We only think when we are confronted with problems
John Dewey

Everyone has the potential to give something back
Princess Diana

A day wasted on others is not wasted on one's self
Charles Dickens

Luck is not chance, it's toil. Fortune's expensive smile is earned.
Emily Dickinson

Life is like a coin. You can spend it any way you wish, but you only spend it once.
Lillian Dickson

There is a gigantic difference between having a great deal of money and being rich
Marlene Dietrich

It's the friends that you can call at 4 AM that matter
Marlene Dietrich

Perfecting oneself is as much unlearning as it is learning
Edsger Dijkstra

You can't test courage cautiously
Annie Dillard

How we spend our days is how we spend our lives
Annie Dillard

To be a person is to have a story to tell
Isak Dinesen

There's been nothing but discipline, discipline, discipline all my life
Celine Dion

When I begin to feel the heat, I begin to see the light
Everett Dirkson

It's not hard to make decisions when you know what your values are
Roy Disney

Our greatest natural resource is the minds of our children
Walt Disney

If you can dream it, you can do it
> *Walt Disney*

All our dreams can come true, if we have the courage to pursue them
> *Walt Disney*

It's fun to do the impossible
> *Walt Disney*

The way to get started is to quit talking and begin doing
> *Walt Disney*

Laughter is America's most important export
> *Walt Disney*

The secret to success is constancy to purpose
> *Benjamin Disraeli*

Patience is a necessary ingredient of genius
> *Benjamin Disraeli*

There is no wisdom like frankness
> *Benjamin Disraeli*

The fool wonders. The wise man asks.
> *Benjamin Disraeli*

Enthusiasm is that secret and harmonious spirit which hovers over the production of genius
> *Isaac Disraeli*

Success is never permanent, and failure is never final
> *Mike Ditka*

You're never a loser until you quit trying
> *Mike Ditka*

I don't think that anything is unrealistic if you believe you can do it
> *Mike Ditka*

I live the life I love and love the life I live
> *Willie Dixon*

Learning the value of silence is learning to listen to reality
> *Thomas Dobush*

It is important to make room in your mind for other living things
> *Thomas Dobush*

Your health is your most important form of wealth
Maria Dolgova

The man who follows a crowd will never be followed by a crowd
R. S.Donnell

The perfect is the enemy of the good
William Donovan

Beauty is our salvation
Dostoevskij

If there is no struggle, there is no progress
Frederick Douglas

People might not get all that they work for in this world, but they must certainly work for all they get
Frederick Douglass

The lesson is that you can still make mistakes and be forgiven
Robert Downey, Jr.

You don't have to act as if you care; you just have to care enough to act
Richard Dreyfuss

Management is doing things right; leadership is doing the right things
Peter Drucker

The only thing we know about the future is that it will be different
Peter Drucker

The best way to predict the future is to create it
Peter Drucker

Manage as if you need your employees more than they need you
Peter Drucker

The most important thing in communication is hearing what isn't said
Peter Drucker

There are limits to material growth, but there are no limits to inner enlightenment
Wayne Dyer

Try viewing everyone who comes into your life as a teacher
Wayne Dyer

It is never crowded along the extra mile
> *Wayne Dyer*

When you judge another, you do not define them, you define yourself
> *Wayne Dyer*

Be miserable. Or motivate yourself. It's always your choice.
> *Wayne Dyer*

Go for it now. The future is promised to no one
> *Wayne Dyer*

When you change the way you look at things, the things you look at change
> *Wayne Dyer*

Doing what you love is the cornerstone of having abundance in your life
> *Wayne Dyer*

Never underestimate your power to change yourself
> *Wayne Dyer*

There are no justified resentments
> *Wayne Dyer*

There are no wrong roads to anywhere
> *Wayne Dyer*

True nobility is not being better than everyone else, it is being better than you used to be
> *Wayne Dyer*

If you have a choice between being right or being kind, always choose kindness
> *Wayne Dyer*

Our deeds follow us, and what we have been makes us what we are
> *John Dykes*

A man is a success if he gets up in the morning and goes to bed at night and in between does what he wants to do
> *Bob Dylan*

If you're not busy being born, you're busy dying
> *Bob Dylan*

E

Fast is fine, but accuracy is everything
Wyatt Earp

Respect your efforts, respect yourself. Self-respect leads to self-discipline.
Clint Eastwood

You can never achieve anything without getting in someone's way
Abba Eban

One must never look for happiness; one meets it by the way
Isabelle Eberhardt

Life is a whole lot of making do the best you can with the situation at hand
PaulEbert

The price of inaction is far greater than the cost of making a mistake
Meister Eckhart

No day in which you learn something is a complete loss
David Eddings

Opportunity is missed by most people because it is dressed in overalls and looks like work
Thomas Edison

To have a great idea, have a lot of them
Thomas Edison

There are no rules here - we're trying to accomplish something
Thomas Edison

Restlessness and discontent are the first necessities of progress
Thomas Edison

What you are will show in what you do
Thomas Edison

Genius is one percent inspiration and ninety-nine percent perspiration
Thomas Edison

I never did a day's work in my life. It was all fun.
Thomas Edison

If we did the things we are capable of, we would astound ourselves
Thomas Edison

Vision without execution is hallucination
>   *Thomas Edison*

Persistent people begin their success where others end in failure
>   *Edward Eggleston*

As far as possible without surrender, be on good terms with all persons
>   *Max Ehrmann*

Go placidly amid the noise and haste and remember what peace there may be in silence
>   *Max Ehrmann*

Avoid loud and aggressive persons; for they are vexations to the spirit
>   *Max Ehrmann*

If you compare yourself with others you may become bitter or vain
>   *Max Ehrmann*

Enjoy your achievements as well as your plans
>   *Max Ehrmann*

Take kindly the counsel of the years, gracefully surrendering the things of youth
>   *Max Ehrmann*

Many fears are born of fatigue and loneliness
>   *Max Ehrmann*

Beyond a wholesome discipline be gentle with yourself
>   *Max Ehrmann*

You are a child of the universe no less than the trees and the stars
>   *Max Ehrmann*

be at peace with your soul, it is still a beautiful world
>   *Max Ehrmann*

Problems cannot be solved by the same level of thinking that created them
>   *Albert Einstein*

Imagination is more important than knowledge. Knowledge is limited.
>   *Albert Einstein*

Not everything that counts can be counted, and not everything that can be counted counts
Albert Einstein

Your imagination is your preview of life's coming attractions
Albert Einstein

I do not consider myself to be especially smarter than any other person, but I do have a particularly vivid imagination
Albert Einstein

Weakness of attitude becomes weakness of character
Albert Einstein

I never think of the future - it comes soon enough
Albert Einstein

Bureaucracy is the death of all sound work
Albert Einstein

Intellectual growth should commence at birth and cease only at death
Albert Einstein

Mastery demands all of a person
Albert Einstein

In the middle of difficulty, lies opportunity
Albert Einstein

Relativity applies to physics, not ethics
Albert Einstein

Look deep into nature and you will understand everything better
Albert Einstein

You have to learn the rules of the game. And then you have to play better than anyone else
AlbertEinstein

Great spirits have always encountered violent opposition from mediocre minds
AlbertEinstein

A people that values its privileges above its principles soon loses both
Dwight Eisenhower

Plans are nothing; planning is everything
Dwight Eisenhower

Plans are useless, but planning is indispensable
    Dwight Eisenhower

If you want total security, go to prison. The only thing lacking ... is freedom
    Dwight Eisenhower

The search for a scapegoat is the easiest of all hunting expeditions
    Dwight Eisenhower

We are the ones we've been waiting for
    Hopi elders

What do we live for, if not to make life less difficult for each other
    George Eliot

It is never too late to be what you might have been
    George Eliot

One must be poor to know the luxury of giving
    George Eliot

Only those who will risk going too far can possibly find out how far one can go
    TS Eliot

In the middle of difficulty lies opportunity
    DukeEllington

Perseverance is not a long race; it is many short races one after another
    Walter Elliott

It is on our failures that we base a new and different and better success
    Havelock Ellis

When you innovate, you've got to be prepared for everyone telling you you're nuts
    Larry Ellison

The only person you are destined to become is the person you decide to be
    Ralph Emerson

Men love to wonder, and that is the seed of science
    Ralph Emerson

Nothing can bring you peace but yourself
    Ralph Waldo Emerson

All life is an experiment
Ralph Waldo Emerson

God enters by a private door into every individual
Ralph Waldo Emerson

Life is a succession of lessons which must be lived to be understood
Ralph Waldo Emerson

Life is a perpetual instruction in cause and effect
Ralph Waldo Emerson

Life is short, but there is always time for courtesy
Ralph Waldo Emerson

Little minds have little worries, big minds have no time for worries
Ralph Waldo Emerson

Nothing great was ever achieved without enthusiasm
Ralph Waldo Emerson

Happiness is a perfume you cannot pour on others without getting a few drops on yourself
Ralph Waldo Emerson

Enthusiasm is the mother of effort, and without it nothing great was ever achieved
Ralph Waldo Emerson

For every minute you are angry, you lose 60 seconds of happiness
Ralph Waldo Emerson

Every artist was first an amateur
Ralph Waldo Emerson

Once you make a decision, the universe conspires to make it happen
Ralph Waldo Emerson

Self-trust is the first secret of success
Ralph Waldo Emerson

Many eyes go through the meadow, but few see the flowers in it
Ralph Waldo Emerson

A great man is always willing to be little
Ralph Waldo Emerson

The world belongs to the energetic
Ralph Waldo Emerson

What you are, thunders so loud that I cannot hear what you say
Ralph Waldo Emerson

We dare not trust our wit for making our house pleasant to our friend, so we buy ice cream
Ralph WaldoEmerson

Whatever course you decide upon, there is always someone to tell you that you are wrong
Ralph WaldoEmerson

There are always difficulties arising which tempt you to believe that your critics are right
Ralph WaldoEmerson

To map out a course of action and follow it to an end requires courage
Ralph WaldoEmerson

The only true gift is a portion of thyself
Ralph WaldoEmerson

A little integrity is better than any career
Ralph WaldoEmerson

It's not what happens to you, but how you react to it that matters
Epictetus

Only the educated are free
Epictetus

Difficulties are things that show a man's nature
Epictetus

Ruin and recovery are both from within
Epictetus

It is impossible for anyone to learn what he thinks he already knows
Epictetus

I demand more of myself than anyone else could ever expect
Julius Erving

A man's most valuable trait is a judicious sense of what not to believe
Euripides

Question everything. Learn something.
Euripides

Education is a better safeguard of liberty than a standing army
Edward Everett

F

Some people are making such thorough preparations for rainy days that they aren't enjoying today's sunshine
> *William Feather*

Success seems to be largely a matter of hanging on after others have let go
> *WilliamFeather*

No man is a failure who is enjoying life
> *WilliamFeather*

It's how you deal with failure that determines how you achieve success
> *David Feherty*

Talent is a waste without hard work
> *Craig Ferguson*

I believe most things can be said in a few lines
> *Enzo Ferrari*

The test of all knowledge is experiment
> *Richard Feynman*

Good enough never is
> *Debbi Fields*

Leadership is all about unlocking the potential in others
> *Carly Fiorina*

You get the best out of others when you get the best out of yourself
> *Harvey Firestone*

It is only as we develop others that we permanently succeed
> *Harvey Firestone*

Never be bullied into silence.
> *Harvey Firestone*

Accept no one's definition of your life, but define yourself
> *Harvey Firestone*

You're at your best, when you're focused and you're serious and passionate about what you do
> *Derek Fisher*

Easy money - isn't
> *Ken Fisher*

Creativity often consists of merely turning up what is already there
Bernice Fitz-Gibbon

It isn't where you came from; it's where you're going that counts
Ella Fitzgerald

If they don't depend on true evidence, scientists are no better than gossips
Penelope Fitzgerald

I learned the value of hard work by working hard
Margaret Fitzpatrick

He has half the deed done who has made a beginning
Flaccus

You cannot protect yourself from sadness without protecting yourself from happiness
Jonathan Foer

There are three kinds of mathematicians; those that can count and those that can't
Nelson Fong

A dose of adversity is often as needful as a dose of medicine
B.C. Forbes

It's so much easier to do good than to be good
B.C. Forbes

Be the best you can be. Everybody else is already taken.
Evelyn Forbes

Ability will never catch up with the demand for it
Malcolm Forbes

Education's purpose is to replace an empty mind with an open one
Malcolm Forbes

Diamonds are nothing more than chunks of coal that stuck to their jobs
Malcolm Forbes

Too many people overvalue what they are not and undervalue what they are
Malcolm Forbes

If you do not do the thing you fear, the fear controls your life
GlenFord

Obstacles are those frightful things you see when you take your eyes off your goal
>   *Henry Ford*

Anyone who stops learning is old, whether at twenty or eighty
>   *Henry Ford*

One who fears failure limits his activities
>   *Henry Ford*

The only real security that a man will have in this world is a reserve of knowledge
>   *Henry Ford*

You can't build a reputation on what you're going to do
>   *Henry Ford*

If I'd asked customers what they wanted, they would have told me, "A faster horse"
>   *Henry Ford*

Getting ready is the secret of success
>   *Henry Ford*

You can speak well if your tongue can't deliver the message of your heart
>   *John Ford*

We must be willing to let go of the life we planned so as to have the life that is waiting for us   5-12-20
>   *E. Forester*

Don't simply retire from something; have something to retire to
>   *Harry Fosdick*

Normal is not something to aspire to; it's something to get away from
>   *Jodie Foster*

People are not against you, they are merely for themselves
>   *Gene Fowler*

I can control how willing I am to step up if somebody needs me
>   *Michael J. Fox*

Nine tenths of education is encouragement
>   *Anatole France*

To accomplish great things, we must dream as well as act
>   *Anatole France*

If 50 million people say a foolish thing, it is still a foolish thing
Anatole France

It is by acts and not by ideas that people live
Anatole France

Either you get bigger or you get smaller, you can't stand still
Bill France, Sr.

It is in giving that one receives
Saint Francis

Everyone has inside of him a piece of good news
Anne Frank

The final forming of a person's character lies in his own hands
Anne Frank

Nobody need wait a single moment before starting to improve the world
Anne Frank

Everyone has inside him a piece of good news
Anne Frank

The last great freedom of man is the freedom to choose his attitude under any given set of circumstances
Viktor Frankl

Any fool can criticize, condemn, and complain - and most fools do
Ben Franklin

A slip of the foot you may soon recover, but a slip of the tongue you may never get over
Ben Franklin

He that will not apply new remedies must expect new evils
Ben Franklin

Great opportunity is often disguised as hard work
Benjamin Franklin

Employ thy time well, if thy meanest to get leisure
Benjamin Franklin

An investment in knowledge pays the best interest
Benjamin Franklin

It is the first responsibility of every citizen to question authority
Benjamin Franklin

When you're finished changing, you're finished
Benjamin Franklin

Well done, is better than well said
Benjamin Franklin

It is easier to prevent bad habits than to break them
Benjamin Franklin

Where liberty dwells, there is my country
Benjamin Franklin

To be humble to superiors is a duty; to equals, courtesy; to inferiors, nobleness
Benjamin Franklin

Lost time is never found again
Benjamin Franklin

He that is good for making excuses is seldom good for anything else
Benjamin Franklin

The only thing more expensive than education is ignorance
Benjamin Franklin

Thought is action in rehearsal
Sigmund Freud

People have been known to achieve more as a result of working with others than against them
Allan Fromme

The only way around is through
Robert Frost

Happiness makes up in height for what it lacks in length
Robert Frost

Education is the ability to listen to almost anything without losing your temper or your self-confidence
Robert Frost

Integrity is the essence of everything successful
Buckminster Fuller

Dare to be naive
Buckminster Fuller

We are called to be architects of the future, not its victims
BuckminsterFuller

We never know the worth of water 'til the well is dry
  Thomas Fuller 6-30-21

One good head is better than a hundred strong hands
  Thomas Fuller

G

The beginning of wisdom is to desire it
> *Ibn Gabirol*

Words mean nothing. Action is the only thing
> *Ernest Gaines*

You cannot teach a man anything; you can only help him find it within himself
> *Galileo Galilei*

Never underestimate how well you're going to do in your life
> *TomGallagher*

Live as if you were to die tomorrow. Learn as if you were to live forever
> *Mahatma Gandhi*

In a gentle way, you can shake the world
> *Mahatma Gandhi*

In matters of conscience, the law of the majority has no place.
> *Mahatma Gandhi*

A man is but the product of his thoughts. What he thinks he becomes.
> *Mahatma Gandhi*

The only tyrant I accept in this world is the "still small voice" within.
> *Mahatma Gandhi*

Strength does not come from physical capacity. It comes from an indomitable will.
> *Mahatma Gandhi*

I do not want to foresee the future. I am concerned with taking care of the present.
> *Mahatma Gandhi*

My life is my message.
> *Mahatma Gandhi*

The difference between what we do and we are capable of doing would suffice to solve most of the world's problems
> *Mohandas Gandhi*

I am not built for academic writings. Action is my domain.
> *Mohandas Gandhi*

The weak can never forgive. Forgiveness is the attribute of the strong.
> *Mohandas Gandhi*

Strength comes from an indomitable will
> *Mohandas Gandhi*

Action expresses priorities
> *Mohandas Gandhi*

the quality of a product is exactly what the customer says it is
> *Jack Ganssle*

It's not what you take but what you leave behind that defines greatness
> *Edward Gardner*

We must strive to reach that simplicity that lies beyond sophistication
> *John Gardner*

Next in importance to freedom and justice is popular education
> *James Garfield*

Things don't turn up in this world until somebody turns them up
> *James Garfield*

Real leaders are ordinary people with extraordinary determinations
> *John Garns*

Amateurs hope, professionals work
> *Kanin Garson*

Like an ability or a muscle, hearing your inner wisdom is strengthened by doing it
> *Robbie Gass*

Passionate leadership won't succeed if contradictory signals are sent out
> *Bill Gates*

Your most unhappy customers are your greatest source of learning
> *Bill Gates*

Problems are messages
> *Shakti Gawain*

I like nonsense; it wakes up the brain cells
> *Theodor Geisel*

We must not be hampered by yesterday's myths in concentrating on today's needs
    Harold Geneen

Performance is your reality. Forget everything else
    Harold Geneen

There is nothing so fatal to character as half finished tasks
    David LloydGeorge

He who sees the truth, let him proclaim it, without asking who is for it or who is against it
    Henry George

While living, I want to live well
    Geronimo

Life is a lot like jazz. It's best when you improvise.
    George Gershwin

A winning effort begins with preparation
    Joe Gibbs

People who enjoy what they are doing invariably do it well
    JoeGibbs

Out of suffering have emerged the strongest souls
    Khalil Gibran

No matter what accomplishments you make, somebody helps you
    Althea Gibson

The future is here; it just isn't very evenly distributed
    William Gibson

Most quarrels amplify a misunderstanding
    Andre Gide

Believe those who are seeking the truth. Doubt those who find it.
    Andre Gide

Genius is the curiosity of childhood constantly recaptured
    Barrie Gilbert

Knowledge is information activated by thought
    Barrie Gilbert

Loser's visualize the penalties of failure. Winners visualize the rewards of success.
    RobGilbert

Nothing is easy for the unwilling
   Nikki Giovanni

Make decisions from the heart and use your head to make it work out
   SirGirad

A happy life is spent in learning, earning, and yearning
   Lillian Gish

Hard work is a prison sentence only if it does not have meaning
   Malcolm Gladwell

Ideas not coupled with action never become bigger than the brain cells they occupied
   Arnold Glasgow

Not all change is growth, as not all movement is forward
   Ellen Glasgow

Good teaching is one-fourth preparation and three-fourths theater
   Gail Godwin

Before you can do something, you must be something
   Goethe

A great deal of talent is lost to the world for want of a little courage
   Goethe

What happens is not as important as how you react to what happens
   ThaddeusGolas

The squeaking wheel doesn't always get the grease. Sometimes it gets replaced
   Vic Gold

The only thing that overcomes hard luck is hard work.
   Harry Golden

Risk the fall in order to fly
   Karen Goldman

No man really becomes a fool until he stops asking questions
   Barry Goldwater

Every individual matters. Every individual makes a difference.
   Jane Goodall

Your life is yours and yours alone. Rise up and live it.
Terry Goodkind

Courage is like a muscle. We strengthen it with use.
Ruth Gordon

Friendship multiplies the good of life and divides the evil
Baltasar Gracian

A wise man gets more use from his enemies than a fool from his friends
Baltasar Gracian

When a brave man takes a stand, the spines of others are stiffened
Billy Graham

No one can avoid aging, but aging productively is something else
Katharine Graham

Fire is the test of gold; adversity, of strong men
Martha Graham

You'll always miss 100% of the shots you don't take
Wayne Gretzky

The highest compliment that you can pay me is to say that I work hard every day
Wayne Gretzky

Skate to where the puck is going to be, not where it has been
Wayne Gretzky

The difficulty, the ordeal, is to start
Zane Grey

H

The difference between a hero and a coward is one step sideways
Gene Hackman

Asking the right questions takes as much skill as giving the right answers
Robert Half

When one teaches, two learn
Robert Half

Acting on a good idea is better than just having a good idea
RobertHalf

Hard work without talent is a shame, but talent without hard work is a tragedy
RobertHalf

Maturity is knowing when to be immature
RandallHall

The fullness of life is in the hazards of life
Edith Hamilton

The only disability in life is a bad attitude.
Scott Hamilton

You can only find life in the present moment
Thich Nhat Hahn

Words are inadequate to express the truth of ultimate reality
Thich Nhat Hanh

The best way to take care of the future is to take care of the present moment
Thich Nhat Hanh

Love has no meaning without understanding
Thich Nhat Hanh

Life is a walk and we should be able to enjoy each step that we take
Thich Nhat Hanh

My actions are my only true belongings
Thich Nhat Hanh

It's wonderful to be alive and to walk on earth
Thich Nhat Hanh

We have more possibilities available in each moment than we realize
>	*Thich Nhat Hanh*

Life is good, without it we'd all be dead.
>	*Hannah*

We will either find a way, or make one
>	*Hannibal*

Big goals get big results. No goals get no results
>	*Mark Hansen*

Whatever you are ready for is ready for you
>	*Mark Hansen*

In imagination, there's no limitation
>	*Mark Hansen*

Our most dangerous tendency is to expect too much of government
>	*Warren Harding*

The time to relax is when you don't have time for it
>	*SydneyHarris*

I have never seen a monument erected to a pessimist
>	*Paul Harvey*

The greatest masterpieces were once only pigments on a palette
>	*Henry Haskins*

Never forget that it is the spirit with which you endow your work that makes it useful or futile
>	*Adelaide Hasse*

Courage means going against the majority opinion in the name of truth
>	*Valcav Havel*

Intelligence is the ability to adapt to change
>	*Stephen Hawking*

Quiet people have the loudest minds
>	*Stephen Hawking*

Companies don't innovate; people do
>	*Jeff Hawkins*

The world owes its onward impulses to men ill at ease
>	*Nathaniel Hawthorne*

When a man is no longer anxious to do better than well, he is done for
> *Benjamin Haydon*

Nothing great in the world has ever been accomplished without passion
> *Christian Hebbel*

To do a common thing uncommonly well brings success
> *Henry Heinz*

The easiest way of making money is to stop losing it
> *Robert Heller*

Never ignore a gut feeling, but never believe that it's enough
> *RobertHeller*

Write as well as you can and finish what you start
> *EarnestHemingway*

Every port of refuge has its price
> *Don Henley*

Unleash your best work every day
> *Todd Henry*

An open mind collects more riches than an open purse
> *Will Henry*

As one goes through life one learns that if you don't paddle your own canoe, you don't move
> *Katharine Hepburn*

Without discipline, there is no life at all
> *Katharine Hepburn*

I never lose sight of the fact that just being is fun
> *Katharine Hepburn*

No man steps in the same river twice, for it's not the same river and he's not the same man
> *Heraclitus*

There is great force hidden in a gentle command
> *GeorgeHerbert*

Miracles can happen in your life every day
> *Jeff Herman*

64

The destiny of man is in his own soul
    Herodotus

Laughing at our mistakes can lengthen our own lives. Laughing at someone else's mistakes can shorten it.
    Cullen Hightower

We sometimes get all of the information, but refuse to get the message
    Cullen Hightower

If you do not conquer self, you will be conquered by self
    Napoleon Hill

Patience, persistence and perspiration make an unbeatable combination for success
    Napoleon Hill

The best job goes to the person who can get it done without passing the buck or coming back with excuses
    Napoleon Hill

One sound idea is all you need to achieve success
    Napoleon Hill

Temporary defeat is not failure unless it accepted as such
    Napoleon Hill

What a marvelous thing it is to have a feeling of love in your heart
    Napoleon Hill

All achievements, all earned riches, have their beginning in an idea
    Napoleon Hill

If you cannot do great things, do small things in a great way
    Napoleon Hill

You give before you get
    Napoleon Hill

Most misfortunes are the result of misused time
    Napoleon Hill

Action is the real measure of intelligence
    Napoleon Hill

Effort only fully releases its reward after a person refuses to quit
    Napoleon Hill

It is not the mountain we conquer, but ourselves
>   *Edmund Hillary*

Happiness is not a destination. It is a method of life
>   *Burton Hills*   9-24-20

You control your life by controlling your time
>   *Conrad Hilton*

Successful men keep moving. They make mistakes, but they don't quit.
>   *Conrad Hilton*

Clean out a corner of your mind and creativity will instantly fill it
>   *Dee Hock*

Some things have to be believed to be seen
>   *Ralph Hodgson*

Thinking something does not make it true
>   *Michelle Hodkin*

There is no real freedom without the freedom to fail
>   *Eric Hoffer*

In time of drastic change, it is the learners who inherit the future
>   *Eric Hoffer*

A dog is not 'almost human,' and I know of no greater insult to the canine race than to describe it as such
>   *John Holmes*

Greatness is not where we stand but in what direction we are moving 3-3
>   *Oliver Wendell Holmes*

A mind once stretched by a new idea never regains its original dimensions 2-2-22
>   *Oliver WendellHolmes*

To a great mind, nothing is little
>   *Sherlock Holmes*

There is nothing more deceptive than an obvious fact
>   *Sherlock Holmes*

It is a capital mistake to theorize before one has data
>   *Sherlock Holmes*

It is the province of knowledge to speak, and the privilege of wisdom to listen
> *Oliver Wendell Holmes, Sr.*

No one has ever drowned in sweat
> *Lou Holtz*

The only people that you should ever try to get "even" with are those that have helped you
> *John Honeyfeld*

Change is not made without inconvenience, even from worse to better
> *Richard Hooker*

Goals are the fuel in the furnace of achievement
> *ThomasHopkins*

One accurate measurement is worth a thousand expert opinions
> *Grace Hopper*

Force without wisdom falls of its own weight
> *Horace*

Rule your mind or it will rule you
> *Horace*

Every time you make the hard, correct decision you become a bit more courageous
> *Ben Horowitz*

Good ideas are a dime a dozen, bad ones are free
> *Doug Horton*

Action cures fear, inaction creates terror
> *Doug Horton*

Although gold dust is precious, when it gets in your eyes it obstructs your vision
> *Hsi-Tang*

Every man is a fool for at least five minutes every day. Wisdom consists in not exceeding the limit.
> *Elbert Hubbard*

You can lead a boy to college, but you cannot make him to think
> *Elbert Hubbard*

Get happiness out of your work or you may never know what happiness is
    Elbert Hubbard

We work to become, not to acquire
    Elbert Hubbard

Some people grow under responsibility, others merely swell
    Carl Hubbell

The meaning of life is to give life meaning
    Ken Hudgins

He who opens a school door, closes a prison
    Victor Hugo

Woe to him who believes in nothing
    Victor Hugo

Better to ask twice than to lose your way once
    Hubert Humphrey

It's more important to know your weaknesses than your strengths
    Ray Hunt

Winning isn't everything. Wanting to win is.
    Catfish Hunter

Don't look behind you
    Daniel Hunter

You don't get paid for the most important things that you do in life
    Steve Hunter

Money can't buy happiness, but poverty can't either
    Steven Hunter

While wisdom occasionally evades the aged, it is a stranger amongst the young
    Steven Hunter

It is better to yield your right of way than be hit by someone in a hurry
    Steven Hunter

You can choose your attitude. I choose to be optimistic
    Steven Hunter

It is better to be clever than a genius, because genius is often narrowly focused
> *Steven Hunter*

You have to feed your ego some, just don't over indulge
> *Steven Hunter*

We all imagine things - happy people imagine good things
> *Steven Hunter*

The mighty and the lowly all bend to the wind, it is just a matter of degree
> *Steven Hunter*

In stormy times, be the eye of the storm
> *Steven Hunter*

Lying trades short term gain for long term pain
> *Steven Hunter*

Your peace of mind comes from your mind
> *Steven Hunter*

You will never go anywhere if you stay in your comfort zone
> *Steven Hunter*

Never respond in kind unless responding to kindness
> *Steven Hunter*

Life is too precious to rush through it
> *Steven Hunter*

You are the result of the choices that you have made in your life
> *Steven Hunter*

The word is love. Spread the word.
> *Steven Hunter*

Money talks, but you don't have to listen
> *Steven Hunter*

The more you look for something, the more you will find it. Look for good things.
> *Steven Hunter*

You must constantly prepare for the future or you won't be ready for it
> *Steven Hunter*

A good solution now is better than a great solution too late
Steven Hunter

Don't get mad. Don't get even. Solve the problem.
Steven Hunter

Act like the person you want to be
Steven Hunter

Do the things the person you want to be would do
Steven Hunter

Don't get mad. Don't get even. Get over it. 3-17-21
Steven Hunter

Sometimes it is better to have friends than money
Steven Hunter

Those who give, also receive.
Steven Hunter

Look for beauty, find happiness
Steven Hunter 9-16-20

If you don't invest in your future, you won't have one
Steven Hunter

To achieve total health, you have to work your muscles and relax your mind
Steven Hunter

When you believe in something, you have to take action, even when it is inconvenient
Steven Hunter

Good, but done, is generally better than perfect, but not done
Steven Hunter

If you don't teach others, you aren't reaching your full potential
Steven Hunter

Periodically push up to your limits or your limits will push you down
Steven Hunter

The more I think, the luckier I get
Steven Hunter

Life is a mystery, keep turning the pages
> *Steven Hunter*   5-11-20

If you make it easy to do the right thing, people are more likely to do it
> *Steven Hunter*

I do not strive to be just average
> *Steven Hunter*

When the answer isn't obvious, look beyond the obvious
> *Steven Hunter*

Experience is not what happens to you; it is what you do with what happens to you
> *Aldous Huxley*

Patience and tenacity are worth more than twice their weight of cleverness
> *Thomas Huxley*

Management is nothing more than motivating people
   Lee Iacocca

The speed of the boss is the speed of the team
   Lee Iacocca

In times of great stress or adversity, it's always best to keep busy
   Lee Iacocca

The ability to concentrate and use your time well is everything
   Lee Iacocca 4-13-21

All limits are self imposed
   Icarus

The riskiest thing we can do is just maintain the status quo
   Robert Iger

A battle is lost less through casualties than by discouragement
   Frederick II

The place to be happy is here, the time to be happy is now
   Robert Ingersoll 10-22-20

Great minds have purposes, little minds have wishes
   Washington Irving

J

Genius is initiative on fire
Holbrook Jackson

I do not believe that you can do today's job with yesterday's methods
Nelson Jackson

Always keep an open mind and a compassionate heart
Phil Jackson

I wouldn't have won as much as I did if I had worried about failing
Reggie Jackson

It is all right letting yourself go, as long as you can get yourself back
Mick Jagger

The art of being wise is the art of knowing what to overlook
William James

The greatest use of life is to spend it for something that will outlast it
William James

Act as if what you do makes a difference. It does.
William James

The only competition worthy a wise man is with himself
Anna Jameson

The only way to live is to accept each minute as an unrepeatable miracle
Storm Jameson

Feel the fear and do it anyway
Susan Jeffers

The harder I work, the luckier I get
Thomas Jefferson

In manners of style, swim with the current; in manners of principle, stand like a rock
Thomas Jefferson

Honesty is the first chapter of the book of wisdom
Thomas Jefferson

Those who hammer their guns into plows will plow for those who do not
>	*Thomas Jefferson*

Learn to see in another's calamity the ills that you should avoid
>	*Thomas Jefferson*

Pride costs us more than hunger, thirst, and cold
>	*Thomas Jefferson*

One man with courage is a majority
>	*Thomas Jefferson*

Nothing on earth can help the man with the wrong mental attitude
>	*Thomas Jefferson* 10-19-20

The boisterous sea of liberty is never without a wave
>	*ThomasJefferson*

It is neither wealth nor splendor; but tranquility and occupation which give happiness
>	*ThomasJefferson*

A good name, like good will, is got by many actions and lost by one
>	*Lord Jeffery*

Forgiveness is the needle that knows how to mend
>	*Jewel* 8-3-20

I want to put a ding in the universe
>	*Steve Jobs*

Your time is limited, so don't waste it living someone else's life
>	*Steve Jobs*

Innovation distinguishes between a leader and a follower
>	*Steve Jobs*

Quality is more important than quantity.
>	*Steve Jobs*

Be a yardstick of quality
>	*Steve Jobs*

Deciding what not to do is as important as deciding what to do
>	*Steve Jobs* 12-8-20

Concern yourself not with what you tried and failed in, but with what is still possible for you to do
>	*Pope John XXIII* 9-7-22

Man exists in a world of his own creation
Alexander Bryan Johnson

To jump occasionally into the pit is common to all who visit the mountain
Alexander Bryan Johnson

The clash of ideas is the sound of freedom
Lady Bird Johnson

The noblest search is the search for excellence
Lyndon Johnson

Nothing will ever be attempted if all possible objections must first be overcome
Samuel Johnson

Self-confidence is the first requisite to great undertakings
Samuel Johnson

The true measure of a man is how he treats someone who can do him absolutely no good
Samuel Johnson

Clear your mind of can't
Samuel Johnson

Great works are performed not by strength, but perseverance
Samuel Johnson

The most profound statements are often said in silence
Lynn Johnston

When you get something for nothing, you just haven't been billed for it yet
Franklin Jones

If fear is cultivated, it will become stronger
John Paul Jones

Everyone has talent. What is rare is the courage to follow that talent to the dark place where it leads.
Erica Jong

If you don't risk anything, you risk even more
Erica Jong

Wisdom is knowing what to do; virtue is doing it
David Jordan

You have to expect things of yourself before you can do them
    Michael Jordan

I built my talents on the shoulders of someone else's talent
    Michael Jordan

I've failed over and over and over again in my life, and that is why I succeed
    Michael Jordan

Always turn a negative situation into a positive situation
    Michael Jordan

Talent wins games, but teamwork and intelligence wins championships
    Michael Jordan

Age is no barrier. It's a limitation you put on your mind.
    Jackie Joyner-Kersee

The shoe that fits one person pinches another
    Carl Jung

Your vision will become clear only when you can look into your own heart
    Carl Jung

He conquers twice who conquers himself in victory
    Jyrus

K

You can't stop the waves, but you can learn to surf 5-19-22
Jon Kabat-zinn

A book must be the axe for the frozen sea within us
Franz Kafka

Start with what is right rather than what is acceptable 3-14-21
Franz Kafka

When your work speaks for itself, don't interrupt
Henry Kaiser 10-31-20

Be open-minded, but not so open-minded that your brains fall out
Stephen Kallis, Jr.

If you are not working on important things, you are wasting your time
Dean Kamen

An empty canvas is a living wonder
Wassily Kandinsky

Is beautiful what is inwardly beautiful
Wassily Kandinsky

We can judge the heart of a man by his treatment of animals
Immanuel Kant

Everything can look like a failure in the middle
Rosabeth Kanter

Small wins, small projects, small differences often make huge differences
Rosabeth Kanter

Character, like a photograph, developes in darkness
Yousuf Karsh

Money is like oxygen: Good idea to have enough, but it's not the target
Eugene Kaspersky

You have to let people challenge your ideas
Tom Kastern

Life is a great big canvas; throw all the paint on it you can
Danny Kaye

If someone will lead, 99% of the people will follow
Sam Kazarian

College isn't the place to go for ideas
Helen Keller

The best and most beautiful things in the world cannot be seen or even touched
Helen Keller

The world is full of suffering. It is also full of overcoming it.
Helen Keller

Life is either a daring adventure or nothing
Helen Keller

Security is mostly a superstition. It does not exist in nature.
Helen Keller

Optimism is the faith that leads to achievement
Helen Keller

The only thing worse than being blind is having sight but no vision
Helen Keller

One can never consent to creep when feels an impulse to soar
Helen Keller

It is hard to fight an enemy who has outposts in your head
Sally Kempton

Efforts and courage are not enough without purpose and direction
John Kennedy

The time to repair the roof is when the sun is shining
John Kennedy

Only those who dare to fail greatly can ever achieve greatly
John Kennedy

The war against hunger is truly mankind's war of liberation
John Kennedy

Compromise does not mean cowardice
John Kennedy

Change is the law of life
John Kennedy

A child miseducated is a child lost
 John Kennedy

Civility is not a sign of weakness
 John Kennedy

No problem of human destiny is beyond human beings
 John Kennedy

Those who dare to fail miserably can achieve greatly
 Robert Kennedy

Life isn't a matter of milestones, but of moments
 Rose Kennedy

He who angers you conquers you
 Elizabeth Kenny

Life is a succession of moments; to live each one is to succeed
 Corita Kent

I prefer the sharpest criticism of a single intelligent man to the thoughtless approval of the masses
 Johannes Kepler

Education is too important to be left solely to the educators
 Francis Keppel

You have to learn how to win and not run away when you lose
 Nancy Kerrigan

Life is a team sport
 Brad Keselowski

Flattery is like chewing gum. Enjoy it, but don't swallow it.
 Hank Ketcham

The difficulty lies not so much in developing new ideas as in escaping from the old ones
 John Keynes

When the facts change, I change my mind
 John Keynes

To be upset over what you don't have is to waste what you do have
 Ken Keys, Jr.

My experience tells me that the hard road is almost always the right road
 Shahid Khan

Procrastination is opportunity's assassin
    Victor Kiam

Life is not a problem to be solved, but a reality to be experienced
    Soren Kierkegaard 5-13-20

There is never a perfect time for anything, but there is a right time for everything 5-13-20
    Christopher Kimball

High achievement always takes place in the framework of high expectation
    Jack Kinder

The beautiful thing about learning is nobody can take it away from you
    B.B. King

If you're small, you'd better be a winner
    Billie Jean King

Our lives start to end the day we become silent about things that matter
    Martin Luther King

What separates the talented individual from the successful one is a lot of hard work
    Stephen King

When asked, 'How do you write?' I invariably answer, 'one word at a time.'
    Stephen King

The time is always right to do what is right
    Martin Luther King, Jr.

Either we go up together or we go down together
    Martin Luther King, Jr. 7-10-20

Injustice anywhere is a threat to justice everywhere
    Martin Luther King, Jr.

Freedom is rarely gained without sacrifice and self-denial
    Martin Luther King, Jr.

People with good intentions but limited understanding are more dangerous than people with total ill will
    Martin Luther King, Jr.

All we need to make us happy is something to be enthusiastic about
Charles Kingsley

Gardens are not made by sitting in the shade
Rudyard Kipling

The task of the leader is to get his people from where they are to where they have not been
Henry Kissinger

A leader does not deserve the name unless he is willing occasionally to stand alone
Henry Kissinger

In crises the most daring course is often the safest
Henry Kissinger

History is made by individuals
Henry Kissinger

A single day is enough to make us a little larger
Paul Klee

Work is the medicine of the soul
Grenville Kleiser

Confidence is preparation. Everything else is beyond your control
Richard Kline

Done is good
Dan Klumpner

Every mistake that I made came because I didn't take the time to get the facts
Charles Knight

Good leaders make people feel they're at the heart of things
Fred Kofman

The important thing is not to retreat; you have to master yourself
Olga Korbut

Honor isn't about making the right choices. It's about dealing with the consequences.
Midori Koto

Plant goodness to harvest goodness
BaranKorkmaz

Leadership creates the system that managers manage
>   *John Kotter*

Each day provides countless chances to make a difference
>   *Jim Kouzes*

A new idea is like a child. It's easier to conceive than to deliver
>   *Ted Koysis*

Pick battles big enough to matter, small enough to win
>   *JonathonKozol*

Middleness is the very enemy of the bold
>   *Charles Krauthammer*

You only have one thing to sell in life, and that's yourself
>   *Henry Kravis*

When the flower blooms, the bees come uninvited
>   *RamaKrishna*

Luck is a dividend of sweat
>   *Ray Kroc*

L

Victory is won not in miles but in inches
    Luis L'Amour

Inspiration usually comes during work, rather than before it
    Madeleine L'Engle

Play every game as if it is your last one
    Guy Lafleur

I hate to work out, but I like the results, so I do it
    Jack LaLanne

Every day, think as you wake up, today I am fortunate to be alive, I have a precious human life, I am not going to waste it
    Dalai Lama

If you want others to be happy, practice compassion. If you want to be happy, practice compassion
    Dalai Lama

My religion is kindness
    Dalai Lama

If your heart has peace, nothing can disturb you
    Dalai Lama

The atrocities of the few do not condemn the many
    Dalai Lama

Being happy is more fun than being angry
    Dalai Lama

When performed with feeling and respect for human values, all activities become constructive
    Dalai Lama

True compassion brings with it the appeasement of internal tensions
    Dalai Lama

Anger and hatred are the main obstacles to compassion
    Dalai Lama

An outburst of anger is an infallible sign of weakness
    Dalai Lama

Anger blinds you to the truth
    Dalai Lama

In order to carry a positive action, we must develop a positive vision
> *Dalai Lama*

A year from now you will wish you had started today
> *Karen Lamb*

Joy is the best makeup
> *Anne Lamott*

Don't accept your dog's admiration as conclusive evidence that you are wonderful
> *Ann Landers*

Maturity is the ability to do a job whether or not you are supervised
> *Ann Landers*

The naked truth is always better than the best dressed lie
> *Ann Landers*

It is not what you do for your children but what you have taught them to do for themselves
> *Ann Landers*

Anyone who says the days of opportunity are over is copping out
> *Ann Landers*

Maturity: Be able to stick with a job until it is finished
> *Ann Landers*

Nobody ever drowned in their own sweat
> *Ann Landers*

If you listen to too much advice you may wind up making other people's mistakes
> *Ann Landers*

If you are prepared, you will be confident and will do the job
> *Tom Landry*

Happiness is something that comes into our lives through doors we don't even remember open
> *Rose Lane*

Rare is the person who can weigh the faults of others without putting his thumb on the scale
> *Byron Langenfield*

Forget regret, or life is yours to miss
> *Jonathan Larson*

My success is based on persistence, not luck
> *Estee Lauder*

I could tell where the lamplighter had been by the trail he left behind
> *Harry Lauder*

It may be that those who do most dream most
> *Stephen Leacock*

It may be those who do most, dream most
> *StephenLeacock*

Life is made up of small pleasures. Happiness is made up of those tiny successes.
> *Norman Lear*

A satisfied customer is the best business strategy of all
> *Michael LeBoeuf*

Waste your time and you've lost a part of your life
> *Michael LeBoeuf*

Knowing is not enough; we must apply
> *Bruce Lee*

Willing is not enough; we must do
> *Bruce Lee*

Be happy, but never satisfied
> *Bruce Lee*

Mistakes are always forgivable, if one has the courage to admit them
> *Bruce Lee*

Love is like a friendship caught on fire
> *Bruce Lee*

Adapt what is useful, reject what is useless, and add what is specifically your own
> *Bruce Lee*

A goal is not always meant to be reached, it often serves simply as something to aim at
> *Bruce Lee*

Do not pray for an easy life, pray for the strength to endure a difficult one
> *Bruce Lee*

All types of knowledge lead to self-knowledge
    BruceLee

The only thing that doesn't abide by majority rule is a person's conscience
    Harper Lee

Ambition without knowledge is like a boat on dry land
    Mark Lee

I do not trust a man to control others who cannot control himself
    Robert E. Lee

Failure seldom stops you. What stops you is the fear of failure
    Jack Lemmon

Death ends a life, not a relationship
    Jack Lemmon

Within our dreams and aspirations we find our opportunities
    Sugar Ray Leonard

There are some who can live without wild things, and some who cannot
    Aldo Leopold

Conservation is a state of harmony between men and land
    Aldo Leopold

Many a calm river begins as a turbulent waterfall
    Mikhail Lermontov

Don't watch the clock; do what it does. Keep going.
    Samuel Levenson

Time is our most precious asset; we should invest it wisely
    MichaelLevy

Yearn to understand first and to be understood second
    Beca Lewis

The task of the modern educator is not to cut down jungles, but to irrigate deserts
    C.S. Lewis

You are never too old to set another goal or to dream a new dream
    C.S. Lewis

You only live once - but if you work it right, once is enough.
    Joe Lewis

Nobody will believe in you unless you believe in yourself
Liberace

Everything that people create is a projection of what's inside them
Stuart Lichtman

Give me six hours to chop down a tree and I will spend the first four sharpening the axe
Abraham Lincoln

You cannot escape the responsibility of tomorrow by evading it today
Abraham Lincoln

Most folks are about as happy as they make up their minds to be
Abraham Lincoln 8- 17-20

The best thing about the future is that it only comes one day at a time
Abraham Lincoln

Nearly all men can stand adversity, but if you want to test a man's character, give him power
Abraham Lincoln

Determine that the thing can and shall be done, and then we shall find the way
Abraham Lincoln

When I do good, I feel good. When I do bad, I feel bad.
Abraham Lincoln

Whatever you are, be a good one
Abraham Lincoln

No man has a good enough memory to make a successful liar
Abraham Lincoln

And in the end, it's not the years in your life that count. It's the life in your years
Abraham Lincoln

I am a slow walker, but I never walk backwards
Abraham Lincoln

Things may come to those who wait, but only the things left by those who hustle
Abraham Lincoln

We should be too big to take offense and too noble to give it
Abraham Lincoln

My father taught me to work; he did not teach me to love it
Abraham Lincoln

Commitment is what transforms a promise into reality
Abraham Lincoln

He has a right to criticize who has a heart to help
Abraham Lincoln

Life without risk is not worth living
Charles Lindbergh

Things seem to turn out best for those who make the best of the way things turn out   6-9-20
Art Linkletter

A prudent person avoids unpleasant things; but a wise man overcomes them
Michael Lipman

Industry is a better horse to ride than genius
Walter Lippmann

One thought driven home is better than three left on base
JamesLiter

The actions of men are the best interpreter of their thoughts
John Locke

It is almost impossible to overestimate the unimportance of most things   3-26-21
John Logue

The harder you work, the harder it is to surrender
Vince Lombardi

The dictionary is the only place that success comes before work
Vince Lombardi 6-3-22

Hard work is the price we must pay for success
Vince Lombardi

I think you can accomplish anything if you're willing to pay the price
Vince Lombardi

Sooner or later the man who wins, is the man who thinks he can
Vince Lombardi

Winning is a habit. Unfortunately, so is losing.
Vince Lombardi

Confidence is contagious. So is lack of confidence.
Vince Lombardi

Leaders aren't born; they are made - through hard work
Vince Lombardi

Success demands singleness of purpose
Vince Lombardi

You can't wait for inspiration. You have to go after it with a club
Jack London

He that respects himself is safe from others. He wears a coat of mail that none can pierce
Henry Longfellow

Be truthful; nature only sides with truth
Adolf Loos

Mistakes are part of the dues that one pays for a full life
Sophia Loren

Putting off an easy thing makes it hard. Putting off a hard thing makes it impossible
George Lorimer

All speaking is public speaking whether it's to one person or a thousand
RogerLove

Take things in single steps - work toward solutions
James Lovell

We're all stumbling towards the light with varying degrees of grace at any given moment
BoLozoff

A man who wants to lead the orchestra must turn his back on the crowd
Max Lucado

You can't do it unless you imagine it
GeorgeLucas

Courage is the ladder on which all the other virtues mount
    Clare Luce

Flexible people never get bent out of shape
    Robert Ludlum 9-28-20

I am bigger than anything that can happen to me
    Charles Lummis

To get anywhere, strike out for somewhere, or you'll get nowhere
    Martha Lupton

The best way to get through tough times is to surround yourself with positive people
    Marcus Luttrell

If you spend 13 minutes per year trying to predict the economy, you have wasted 10 minutes
    PeterLynch

Today is the only cash you have, so spend it wisely
    Kim Lyons 6-16-20

M

There is no security on this earth; there is only opportunity
   Douglas MacArthur

The measure of a man's real character is what he would do if he knew he never would be found out
   Thomas Macaulay

Ambiguous commitment produces mediocre results
   Harvey Mackay

People begin to become successful the minute they decide to be
   HarveyMacKay

Coaches have to watch for what they don't want to see and listen to what they don't want to hear
   John Madden

Computers can figure out all kinds of problems, except the things in the world that just don't add up
   James Magary

Growth depends on being always in motioning way or another
   Norman Mailer

Teach your tongue to say "I do not know," and you shall progress
   Maimonides

To change a habit, make a conscious decision, then act out the new behavior
   Maxwell Maltz

Low self-esteem is like driving through life with your handbrake on
   Maxwell Maltz

You make mistakes. Mistakes don't make you.
   MaxwellMaltz

The greatest glory in living lies not in never falling, but in rising every time we fall
   Nelson Mandela

Do not listen to those who weep and complain, for their disease is contagious
   Og Mandino

I will strain my potential until it cries for mercy
   Og Mandino

Act now. For now is all you have.
Og Mandino

Action is the food and drink which will nourish my success.
Og Mandino

Action will destroy your procrastination.
Og Mandino

All men must stumble often to reach the truth.
Og Mandino

All your problems, discouragements, and heartaches are, in truth, great opportunities in disguise.
Og Mandino

Always raise your goals as soon as they are attained.
Og Mandino

Any act with practice becomes easy.
Og Mandino

Bad habits must be destroyed and new furrows prepared for good seed.
Og Mandino

Bathe me in good habits that the bad ones may drown.
Og Mandino

Be prepared to control whatever personality awakes in you each day.
Og Mandino

Become master of yourself.
Og Mandino

Cherish each hour of this day for it can never return.
Og Mandino 6-29-20

Chuckle and your burdens will be lightened.
Og Mandino 5-19-20

Concentrate your energy on the challenge of the moment.
Og Mandino

Consider each obstacle as a mere detour to your goal and a challenge to your profession.

Og Mandino

Cultivate the habit of laughter.
Og Mandino

Drive a bad habit from your life and replace it with one which will bring you closer to success.
Og Mandino

Enjoy today's happiness today.
Og Mandino

Fulfill today's duties today.
Og Mandino

Good habits are the key to all success.
Og Mandino

Grant me compassion for weaknesses in others.
Og Mandino

I will acknowledge rewards for they are my due; yet I will welcome obstacles for they are my challenge.
Og Mandino

I will command, and I will obey mine own command.
Og Mandino

I will form good habits and become their slave.
Og Mandino

If you must be a slave to habit, then be a slave to good habits.
Og Mandino

If you waste today, you destroy the last page of your life.
Og Mandino

Laugh at your successes and they will shrink to their true value.
Og Mandino

Laugh at yourself for man is most comical when he takes himself too seriously.
Og Mandino

Lift up a friend in need.
Og Mandino

Make every hour count and trade each minute only for something of value.
> *Og Mandino*

Never will I labor to be happy; rather will I remain too busy to be sad.
> *Og Mandino*

Only a habit can subdue another habit.
> *Og Mandino*

Practice the art of patience for nature never acts in haste.
> *Og Mandino*

Success comes to those willing to work a little bit harder than the rest. 7-1-21
> *Og Mandino*

The prizes of life are at the end of each journey, not near the beginning.
> *Og Mandino*

To multiply your value you must multiply your actions.
> *Og Mandino*

To surpass the deeds of others is unimportant; to surpass your own deeds is all. 5-18-21
> *Og Mandino*

True wealth is of the heart, not of the purse.
> *Og Mandino*

With each victory the next struggle becomes less difficult.
> *Og Mandino*

You can accomplish far more than you have, and you will.
> *Og Mandino*

You can overcome seemingly impossible obstacles with ambition.
> *Og Mandino*

You have been given eyes to see and a mind to think.
> *Og Mandino*

You won't know how close success is unless you turn the corner.
> *Og Mandino* 7-1-22

We must be purposely kind and generous or we miss the best part of life's existence
    Horace Mann

What happens to a man is less significant than what happens within him
    Luis Mann

Only eyes washed by tears can see clearly
    Luis Mann

A team is where a boy can prove his courage on his own. A gang is where a coward goes to hide
    Mickey Mantle

A good system shortens the road to the goal
    Orison Marden

Only in quiet waters do things mirror themselves undistorted
    Hans Margolius

Dissatisfaction is the basis of progress
    J. Willard Marriott Sr.

You can't knock on opportunity's door and not be ready
    Bruno Mars

Small deeds done are better than great deeds planned
    Peter Marshall

A different world cannot be built by indifferent people
    PeterMarshall

Excellence is not a skill.It is an attitude.
    Ralph Marston

Conceal a flaw and the world will imagine the worst
    Marcus Valerius Martialis

Perseverance is a great substitute for talent
    Steve Martin

It is far more impressive when others discover your good qualities without your help
    Judith Martin

Admit your errors before someone else exaggerates them
    Andrew Mason

When you try to be all things to all people, you become nothing to everybody

Michael Masterson

There are always flowers for those who want to see them
  Henri Matisse

Derive happiness in oneself from a good day's work
  Henri Matisse
Love is caring about someone more than you care about yourself
  Takashi Matsuoka

There is 'No Better Friend, No Worse Enemy' than a U.S. Marine
  General James "Mad Dog" Mattis

If you refuse to accept anything but the best, you very often get it
  Somerset Maugham

Tradition is a guide and not a jailer
  Somerset Maugham

The most valuable thing I have learned from life is to regret nothing
  Somerset Maugham

Imagination grows by exercise
  Somerset Maugham

We are either the masters or victims of our attitudes 4-23
  John Maxwell

The greatest mistake a person can make is to do nothing
  John Maxwell

Reflective thinking turns experience into insight.
  John Maxwell

You can't be a smart cookie with a crummy attitude
  John Maxwell 9-3-20

A man must be big enough to admit his mistakes and smart enough to profit from them
  John Maxwell

People may hear your words, but they feel your attitude
  John Maxwell 6-18-20

As a leader, the first person I need to lead is me
  John Maxwell

A minute of thought is greater than an hour of talk
  John Maxwell

Have the humility to learn from those around you
John Maxwell

The only safe thing is to take a chance
Elaine May

People get nervous when they don't know what's going on
Glen Mazzara

Change your thoughts and you change the world
Harold McAlindon

It's better to do nothing at all than to do something badly
Mark McCormack

The important thing is to learn something every time you lose
John McEnroe

To succeed in life you need a wishbone, a backbone, and a funny bone.
Reba McEntire

There is no greater joy nor greater reward than to make a fundamental difference in someone's life
Sister MaryMcGeady

Celebrate any progress. Don't wait to get perfect.
Ann McGee Cooper

There is no achievement without goals
Robert McKain

Two men working as a team will produce more than three men working as individuals
William McKinley

Few of us write great novels; all of us live them.
Mignon McLaughlin

Get the best people and train them well
Scott McNealy

Comfort zones are most often expanded through discomfort
PeterMcWilliams

Heroes became heroes flaws and all. You don't have to be perfect to fulfill your dream
PeterMcWilliams

Mistakes show us what we need to learn
: *PeterMcWilliams*

People with new ideas have always been called troublemakers
: *Richelle Mead*

To finish first, you must first finish
: *RickMears*

You can't shake hands with a clenched fist
: *Golda Meir* 10-13-20

Not being beautiful forced me to develop my inner resources
: *Golda Meir*

Whatever was accomplished in this country was accomplished collectively
: *Golda Meir*

Reading is a college that you can and should attend all your life
: *Paul Mellon*

It is better to fail in originality than to succeed in imitation
: *Herman Melville*

A great man is he who does not lose his childlike heart
: *Mencius*

For every complicated problem there is a solution that is simple, direct, understandable and wrong
: *H.L. Mencken*

There's a huge difference between being a good student and being a good learner   8-5-20
: *Nilofer Merchant*

Enthusiasm is the yeast that raises the dough
: *Paul Meyer*

I hope that I may always desire more than I can accomplish
: *Michelangelo*

A man paints with his brains and not with his hands
: *Michelangelo*

Genius is eternal patience
: *Michelangelo*

Character consists of what you do on the third and fourth tries

James Michener

Always accept good fortune with grace and humility
Mark Mika

If you play to win, the game never ends
Stan Mikita

A person may cause evil to others not only by his actions, but by his inaction
John Stuart Mill

All good things which exist are the fruits of originality
John Stuart Mill

You hardly ever get more than you try to get
George Miller

Good happens
Sue Miller

Before you can see the light, you have to deal with the darkness
DanMillman

Don't ever think you have learned enough or life will throw you some hard lessons
DanMillman

The things that make me different are the things that make me
A.A. Milne

Making the complicated simple, awesomely simple, that's creativity.
Charles Mingus

There are things to confess that enrich the world, and things that need not be said
Joni Mitchell

Life's under no obligation to give us what we expect
Margaret Mitchell

There isn't any pleasing some people. The trick is to stop trying.
Robert Mitchum

Success can corrupt; usefulness can only exalt
Dmitri Mitropolous

I never ran 1,000 miles. I ran one mile 1,000 times
Stu Mittleman

A good listener is not only popular everywhere, but after a while, he gets to know something
    Wilson Mizner

You don't necessarily live for the moment, you live for hope
    Isaac Mizrahi

Help others get ahead. You will always stand taller with someone on your shoulders
    Bob Moawad

The idea is to die young as late as possible
    Ashley Montagu

Civility costs nothing and buys everything
    Mary Montagu

Expect problems and eat them for breakfast
    Alfred Montapert

You are the architect and builder of your own life
    Alfred Montapert

The first step toward getting somewhere is to decide that you are not going to stay where you are
    J.P. Morgan

There is only one success – to be able to spend your life in your own way
    Christopher Morley

No one else will ever see life through my eyes
    Christopher Morley

Happiness is like a pair of eyeglasses correcting your spiritual vision
    Lloyd Morris

It's not always that we need to do more, but rather that we need to focus on less
    Nathan Morris

The leader is the person who brings a little magic to the moment
    Denise Morrison

It is better to lead change than be a victim of it
    Denise Morrison

The irony of commitment is that it's deeply liberating
    Anne Morriss

The minute you're not true to yourself, you're in trouble
Georgette Mosbacher

Deeds, not stones are the true monuments of the great
John Motley

I pay no attention whatever to anybody's praise or blame
Wolfgang Mozart

Climb the mountains and get their good tidings
John Muir

In wilderness is the preservation of the world
John Muir

The power of imagination makes us infinite
John Muir

In every walk with nature, one receives far more than he seeks
John Muir

A certain amount of opposition is a great help to a man
Lewis Mumford

Humor is our way of defending ourselves from life's absurdities
Lewis Mumford

The secret of your future is hidden in your daily routine
Mike Murdock

Cheerfulness is the principle ingredient in the composition of health
Arthur Murphy

Everyone is a prisoner of his own experiences
Edward Murrow

No one can eliminate prejudices - just recognize them
Edward Murrow

N

Trends, like horses, are easier to ride in the direction they are going
    John Naisbitt

If you aren't going all the way, why go at all?
    Joe Namath

You never have any fun out of the things you haven't done
    Thomas Nash

No man can think clearly when his fists are clenched
    George Nathan

Clarity of purpose gives you the mental and physical strength to achieve your goal
    Martina Navratilova

A strong positive mental attitude will create more miracles than any wonder drug
    Patricia Neal

Strong people admit their mistakes, laugh at them, learn from them
    Richard Needham

When everyone thinks alike, everyone is likely to be wrong
    Humphrey Neill

Once you replace negative thoughts with positive ones, you'll start having positive results
    Willie Nelson

I quit being afraid when my first venture failed and the sky didn't fall down
    Al Neuharth

Making tough choices doesn't build character - it reveals it
    C.W. Nevius

Don't ever be afraid to admit you were wrong. It's saying you're wiser now than before
    Robert Newell

Tact is the art of making a point without making an enemy
    Isaac Newton

True progress in science begins with three magic words - I was wrong
    Eric Nichols

Resolve never to quit, never to give up, no matter what the situation
Jack Nicklaus

Don't be too proud to take lessons. I'm not.
Jack Nicklaus

Watch every detail that affects the accuracy of your work
Arthur Nielsen

He who has a strong enough why can bear almost any how
Fredrich Nietzsche

There are no facts, only interpretations
Friedrich Nietzsche

One's own self is well hidden from one's own self
Friedrich Nietzsche

It's choice - not chance - that determines your destiny
Jean Nifetch

Life should be a hoot! Blow your horn!
Emmanuel Nigerian

You become what you think about
Earl Nightingale

There is a time when one must decide either to risk everything to fulfill one's dreams or sit for the rest of one's life in the backyard
Earl Nightingale

Unless a person is worth more than they are receiving, they are receiving all that they are worth
Earl Nightingale

You do not raise morale in an organization, it filters down from the top
Earl Nightingale

Anger, hatred, and jealousy don't hurt others; they hurt you
Earl Nightingale

Our attitude to others determines their attitude towards us
Earl Nightingale

I attribute my success to this, I never gave or took an excuse
Florence Nightingale

How very little can be done under the spirit of fear
Florence Nightingale

Life shrinks or expands in proportion to one's courage
    Anais Nin

We don't see things as they are, we see things as we are
    Anais Nin

We don't see things as they are, we see them as we are
    Anais Nin

Good things happen to those who hustle
    Anais Nin

This planet Earth functions not because of us, but in spite of us.
    Swami Nithyananda

Desire and gratitude can never co-exist
    Nithyananda

One of the most dangerous forms of human error is forgetting what one is trying to achieve
    Paul Nitze

Appreciate the moment
    Isamu Noguchi

When you're true to who you are, amazing things happen
    Deborah Norville 9-22-20

Discomfort means nothing to me as long as I can see that the experience will take me to a new level
    Diana Nyad

O

The only way to overcome is to hang in
    Dan O'Brien

Nothing is politically right which is morally wrong
    Daniel O'Connell

Taking stuff makes you weaker. Earning stuff makes you stronger.
    William O'Riley, Jr.

Aim at a high mark and you will hit it
    Annie Oakley

As for our common defense, we reject as false the choice between our safety and our ideals.
    Barack Obama

We will not apologize for our way of life, nor will we waver in its defense.
    Barack Obama

The only durable strength we have is innovation
    Barack Obama

Remember that you are blessed
    Michelle Obama

You must bend down and let someone stand on your shoulders so they can see a better future
    Michelle Obama

Refusing to ask for help when you need it is refusing someone the chance to be helpful 8-19-20
    Ric Ocasek

More strategies fail because they are overripe than because they are premature
    Kenichi Ohmae

I take a simple view of life: Keep your eyes open and get on with it
    Lawrence Olivier

Life is a mystery to be lived not a problem to be solved
    Clive Ollies 9-10-20

Playing safe is only playing
    ChuckOlson

We can't have more time, but we can have more fun
Mike Ong

I am grateful for all the problems that help me grow
Mike Ong

Don't judge yourself by your past; you no longer live there
IfeanyiOnuoha

Teamwork is the secret that makes common people achieve uncommon results
IfeanyiOnuoha

Every challenge you encounter in your life is a fork in the road
IfeanyiOnuoha

In life, you have a choice to be better or bitter
IfeanyiOnuoha 9-23-20

The foolish man seeks happiness in the distance; the wise grows it under his feet
James Oppenheim

To err is human and to blame it on a computer is even more so
Robert Orben

Happiness is a very small desk and a very big wastebasket
Robert Orben

Time flies. It's up to you to be the navigator.
Robert Orben

Forget about style; worry about results
Bobby Orr

To see what's in front of one's nose requires a constant struggle
George Orwell

Creative ideas reside in people's minds but are trapped by fear or rejection
Alex Osborne

Tears at times have all the weight of speech
Ovid

Life doesn't give you all the practice races you need
Jesse Owens

We often take for granted the very things that most deserve our gratitude
> *Cynthia Ozick*

P

If you don't make mistakes, you're not reaching far enough
David Packard

History doesn't teach us what to think, it teaches us how to think
George Packer

Nobody can pull you down like you can
Diamond Dallas Page

Work ethic equals results
Diamond Dallas Page

Don't look back; they may be gaining on you
Satchel Paige

Our greatest enemies, the ones we must fight most often, are within
Thomas Paine

Character is much easier kept than recovered
Thomas Paine

Those who expect to reap the blessings of freedom must undergo the fatigue of supporting it
Thomas Paine

If there must be trouble, let it be in my day, that my child may have peace
Thomas Paine

We have it in our power to make the world over again
Thomas Paine

Know the importance of when and how to say thank you
Arnold Palmer

The most important things you do in life are the ones that look like they can't be done
Arnold Palmer

Happiness is a by product of an effort to make someone else happy
Gretta Palmer

Find peace in where and what you are
Christopher Paolini

A good coach will make his players see what they can be rather than what they are
Ara Parasheghian

You can't teach an old dogma new tricks
Dorothy Parker

The cure for boredom is curiosity. There is no cure for curiosity.
Dorothy Parker

Purpose is what gives life a meaning
Charles Parkhurst

You got to go down a lot of wrong roads to find the right one
Robert Parsons

Smile, it increases your face value
Dolly Parton

If you don't like the road you're walking, start paving another one
Dolly Parton

Find out who you are and do it on purpose
Dolly Parton

The heart has its reasons which reason knows nothing of
Blaise Pascal

Kind words do not cost much. Yet they accomplish much.
Blaise Pascal

Man's greatness lies in his power of thought
Blaise Pascal

Justice without force in powerless; force without justice is tyrannical
Blaise Pascal

The more intelligent a man is, the more originality he discovers in others
Blaise Pascal

Chance favors the prepared mind
LouisPasteur

What we do tomorrow is more important than what we did yesterday
Pankaj Patel

Success without honor is an unseasoned dish; it will satisfy your hunger, but it won't taste good
Joe Paterno

Accept the Challenge, so you may feel the exhilaration of victory
    George Patton

A good plan today is better than a perfect plan tomorrow
    George Patton

You need to overcome the tug of people against you as you reach for high goals
    George Patton

Success is how high you bounce when you hit bottom
    GeorgePatton 4-5-21

The future starts today, not tomorrow
    John Paul II

Don't become a mere recorder of facts, but try to penetrate the mystery of their origin
    Ivan Pavlov

Work transforms talent into genius
    Anna Pavlova

Without a humble but reasonable confidence in your own powers you cannot be successful or happy
    Norman VincentPeale

To live a creative life, we must lose our fear of being wrong
    Joseph Pearce

In the absence of certainty, there is nothing wrong with hope
    Paul Pearsall

Self-acceptance is more important than self-improvement
    Paul Pearsall

All true growth comes from crisis
    Paul Pearsall

One of the secrets of life is to make stepping stones out of stumbling blocks 6-13-20
    Jack Penn

Time is what we want most, but what we use worst
    William Penn

I would never have amounted to anything were it not for adversity
    J.C. Penney

Change is rarely comfortable
Arno Penzias

Life is like a cobweb, not an organization chart
Ross Perot

Inventories can be managed, but people must be led.
Ross Perot

Life is never more fun than when you're the underdog competing against the giants
RossPerot

You've got to be original, because if you're like someone else, what do they need you for?
Bernadette Peters

Celebrate what you want to see more of
Thomas Peters

Leaders don't create followers, they create more leaders
Tom Peters

I have learned that the novice can often see things that the expert overlooks
Tom Peters

Winners are people who have fun - and produce results as a result of their zest
Tom Peters

Big thinking precedes great achievement
Wilfred Peterson

We tire of those pleasures we take, but never of those we give
John Petit-Senn

Winning is only half of it. Having fun is the other half.
Bum Phillips

The only discipline that lasts is self-discipline
BumPhillips

Inspiration exists, but it has to find you working
Pablo Picasso

Computers are useless. They can only give you answers
Pablo Picasso

Everything you can imagine is real
Pablo Picasso

It is your work in life that is your ultimate seduction
Pablo Picasso

I am always doing that which I cannot do, in order that I may learn how to do it
Pablo Picasso

Action is the foundational key to all success
Pablo Picasso

Without solitude, no serious work is possible
Pablo Picasso

Success for the striver washes away the effort of striving
Pindar

Ignorance, the root and the stem of every evil
Plato

Be kind, for everyone you meet is fighting a hard battle
Plato

Never discourage anyone who continually makes progress, no matter how slow
Plato

When men speak ill of thee, live so as nobody may believe them
Plato

The price good men pay for indifference to public affairs is to be ruled by evil men
Plato

Viscosity of credit vs. blame. Credit has low viscosity and spreads out everywhere; blame sticks in one spot
Randy Pleasance

When you are working with good people, it brings good things out of you
Martha Plimpton

Know how to listen, and you will profit even from those who talk badly
Plutarch

There is no secret to success. It is the result of preparation, hard work, and learning from failure
    Colin Powell

Persistent optimism is a force multiplier
    Colin Powell

You only get back what you expect, and if your expectations are low you'll end low
    Colin Powell

Great leaders are almost always great simplifiers
    Colin Powell

Experts often possess more data than judgment
    ColinPowell

Unless I accept my faults, I will most certainly doubt my virtues
    Hugh Prather

When things go wrong, don't go with them
    Elvis Presley

Truth is like the sun. You can shut it out for a time, but it ain'tgoin' away.
    Elvis Presley

A man who limits his interests limits his life
    Vincent Price

You don't stop laughing because you grow old. You grow old because you stop laughing
    Michael Prichard

Without a big picture, we are very small people
    Joel Primack

It takes two to quarrel, but only one to end it
    Matthew Prior

Fear is that little darkroom where negatives are developed
    Michael Pritchard

As you go through life, you'll find you're never be sorry that you were kind
    Herbert Prochnow

The real voyage of discovery consists not in seeking new landscapes but in having new eyes
    Marcel Proust

When you have given nothing, ask for nothing
    Albanian Proverb 8-21-20

It is less of a problem to be poor, than to be dishonest
    Anishinabe proverb

If we wonder often, the gift of knowledge will come
    Arapaho proverb

He who asks questions cannot avoid the answers
    CameroonProverb

Our first teacher is our own heart
    Cheyenne proverb

If you are patient in one moment of anger, you will escape a hundred days of sorrow
    Chinese Proverb

Unless we change direction, we are likely to wind up where we are headed
    Chinese proverb

A child's life is like a piece of paper on which every person leaves a mark
    Chinese proverb

Teachers open the door but you must walk through it yourself
    Chinese Proverb

The gem cannot be polished without friction, nor man perfected without trials
    Chinese Proverb

The palest ink is better than the best memory
    Chinese Proverb

A bit of fragrance clings to the hand that gives flowers
    Chinese Proverb 6-8-20

Talk does not cook rice
    Chinese proverb

Tension is who you think you should be. Relaxation is who you are.
    Chinese proverb

If you plan for one year, plant rice. If you plan for ten years, plant trees. If you plan for 100 years, educate mankind
    ChineseProverb

One rain does not make a crop
Creole proverb

We are known by the tracks we leave
Dakota proverb

A handful of patience is worth more than a bushel of brains
Dutch Proverb

Charity sees the need, not the cause
German Proverb

The wise person has long ears and a short tongue
German Proverb

We do not inherit this land from our ancestors, we borrow it from our children
Haida Indian Proverb

When the character of a man is not clear to you, look at his friends
Japanese proverb

Fall seven times, stand up eight
Japanese Proverb

One kind word can warm three winter months
Japanese Proverb

Cheerfulness is the very flower of health
Japanese Proverb

Force, no matter how concealed, begets resistance
Lakota proverb

When a man moves away from nature his heart becomes hard
Lakota proverb

If the wind will not serve, take to the oars
Latin Proverb

Seek wisdom, not knowledge. Knowledge is of the past, Wisdom is of the future.
Lumbee proverb

If you see no reason for giving thanks, the fault lies in yourself
Minquass proverb

Cherish youth, but trust old age
Pueblo proverb

Whoever gossips to you, will gossip about you
    Spanish proverb 10-15-20

Those who wish to sing, always find a song.
    Swedish Proverb 8-27-20

They are not dead who live in the hearts they leave behind
    Tuscarora proverb

Be honorable yourself if you wish to associate with honorable people 4-21-22
    Welsh Proverb

If you want your dreams to come true, don't over sleep
    Yiddish Proverb

When the student is ready the teacher will appear
    ZenProverb

Spend what's left after saving, instead of saving what's left after spending
    Proverb

You can't turn back the clock. But you can wind it up again.
    Bonnie Prudden 4-24

Tomorrow is not promised to any of us
    Kirby Puckett

If the human mind were simple enough to understand, we'd be too simple to understand it
    Emerson Pugh

Q

Where one door closes, another opens
Don Quixote

R

Thought is useful when it motivates action and a hindrance when it substitutes for action
> *Bill Raeder*

The maintenance of life and the pursuit of happiness are not two separate issues
> *Ayn Rand*

Do not get obsolete like an old technology; keep innovating yourself
> *SukantRatnaker*

Nothing is invented and perfected at the same time
> *John Ray*

You get back what you give out
> *Nancy Reagan*

Information is the oxygen of the modern age
> *Ronald Reagan*

Don't be afraid to see what you see
> *Ronald Reagan*

We are always willing to be trade partners, but never trade patsies
> *Ronald Reagan*

The world must see a country that is morally strong
> *Ronald Reagan*

The person who pays an ounce of principle for a pound of popularity gets badly cheated
> *Ronald Reagan*

Optimism is a choice, and one of the most powerful we can make
> *Ronald Reagan*

Nobody rises to low expectations
> *Ronald Reagan*

A people free to choose will always choose peace
> *Ronald Reagan*

Life is one grand, sweet song, so start the music
> *Ronald Reagan*

When I see trouble coming, I go on up ahead to meet it
> *Bernice Reagon*

Life's challenges are not supposed to paralyze you; they're supposed t help you discover who you are
>   *Bernice Reagon*

When you handle yourself, use your head; when you handle others, use your heart
>   *Donna Reed*

Either you decide to stay in the shallow end of the pool or you go out in the ocean
>   *Christopher Reeve*

Look for the ridiculous in everything, and you will find it
>   *Jules Renard*

It is not easy finding happiness in ourselves, and it is not possible to find it elsewhere
>   *Agnes Repplier*

With education and hard work, it really does not matter where you came from
>   *Condoleezza Rice*

Lying is done with words and also with silence
>   *Adrienne Rich*

The here and now is all we have, and if we play it right it's all we'll need
>   *Ann Richards*

Ingenuity - plus courage, plus work - equals miracles
>   *Bob Richards*

Don't wait for extraordinary circumstance to do good; try to use ordinary situations
>   *Charles Richter*

Courage is doing what you're afraid to do. There can be no courage unless you're scared
>   *Eddie Rickenbacker*

Think things through - then follow through
>   *Eddie Rickenbacker*

Brood about death and you hasten your demise
>   *Eddie Rickenbacker*

Hierarchy is an organization with its face toward the CEO and its back toward the customer
>   *Jonas Ridderstråle*

Great effort springs naturally from a great attitude
Pat Riley

Excellence is the gradual result of always striving to do better
Pat Riley

It is in moments of decision that your destiny is shaped
Anthony Robbins

Let fear be a counselor and not a jailer
Anthony Robbins

Beliefs have the power to create and the power to destroy
AnthonyRobbins

A truly stable system expects the unexpected, is prepared to be disrupted, waits to be transformed.
Tom Robbins

The road called someday leads to the town called nowhere
Tony Robbins

The secret to living is giving
Tony Robbins

A life is not important except in the impact it has on other lives
Jackie Robinson

When a man finds no peace within himself, it is useless to seek it elsewhere
Francois De LaRochefoucauld

If your only goal is to become rich, you will never achieve it
John Rockefeller

Good management consists in showing average people how to do the work of superior people
John Rockefeller

Don't be afraid to give up the good to go for the great
John Rockefeller

Wherever we look upon this earth, opportunities take shape within the problems
Nelson Rockefeller

Build up your weaknesses until they become your strengths
Knute Rockne

Win or lose, do it fairly
Knute Rockne

The end result of kindness is that it draws people to you
Anita Roddick

If you do things well, do them better
AnitaRoddick

I invent nothing. I rediscover
Auguste Rodin

What one person receives without working for, another person must work for without receiving
Adrian Rogers

The good life is a direction, not a state of being
Carl Rogers

Maybe I should listen to myself instead of everyone else
Jim Rogers

Even if you are on the right track, you'll get run over if you just sit there
Will Rogers

Why not go out on a limb? That is where the fruit is
Will Rogers

If you get to thinkin' that you're a person of some influence, try orderin' someone else's dog around
Will Rogers

What the country needs is dirtier fingernails and cleaner minds
Will Rogers

Never miss a good chance to shut up
Will Rogers

Everybody is ignorant, only on different subjects
Will Rogers

People who fly into a rage always make a bad landing
Will Rogers

Get someone else to blow your horn and the sound will carry twice as far
Will Rogers

121

It's not the hours you put in, but what you put into the hours that count 3-30-21
    JamesRohn

Discipline is the bridge between goals and accomplishments
    Jim Rohn

Formal education will make you a living; self-education will make you a fortune
    Jim Rohn

Take care of your body. It's the only place you have to live.
    Jim Rohn

You cannot get all the answers to life from one person or from one source
    Jim Rohn

Sharing makes you bigger than you are
    Jim Rohn

Either run the day or the day runs you
    jim Rohn

Battles are decided by the quartermasters before the first shot is fired
    Edwin Rommel

You gain strength, courage, and confidence by every experience in which you really stop to look fear in the face
    Eleanor Roosevelt

Great minds discuss ideas. Average minds discuss events. Small minds discuss people
    Eleanor Roosevelt

No one can make you inferior without your consent
    Eleanor Roosevelt

The future belongs to those that believe in the beauty of their dreams 10-21-20
    Eleanor Roosevelt

It takes as much energy to wish as it does to plan
    Eleanor Roosevelt

Happiness is not a goal; it is a by-product.
    Eleanor Roosevelt

We must do that which we think we cannot
Eleanor Roosevelt

With the new day comes new strength and new thoughts
Eleanor Roosevelt

When you get to the end of your rope, tie a knot and hang on
Franklin Roosevelt

Happiness lies in the joy of achievement and the thrill of creative effort
Franklin Roosevelt

In the truest sense, freedom cannot be bestowed; it must be achieved
Franklin Roosevelt

To reach a port, we must sail - sail, not tie at anchor - sail, not drift
Franklin Roosevelt

The only limit to our realization of tomorrow will be our doubts of today
Franklin Roosevelt

Do something. If it works, do more of it. If it doesn't, do something else.
Franklin Roosevelt

Do what you can, with what you have, where you are
Theodore Roosevelt

Nine-tenths of wisdom consists in being wise in time
Theodore Roosevelt

Whenever you are asked if you can do a job, tell 'em, "Certainly I can!" - and get busy and find out how to do it
Theodore Roosevelt

The great virtue of my radicalism lies in the fact that I am perfectly ready, if necessary, to be radical on the conservative side
Theodore Roosevelt

The best executive is one who has sense enough to pick good people to do what he wants done, and self-restraint enough to keep from meddling with them while they do it
Theodore Roosevelt

While my interest in natural history has added very little to my sum of achievement, it has added immeasurably to my sum of enjoyment in life
Theodore Roosevelt

Practical efficiency is common, and lofty idealism not uncommon; it is the combination which is necessary, and the combination is rare
Theodore Roosevelt

If I must choose between righteousness and peace, I choose righteousness
Theodore Roosevelt

When you play, play hard; when you work, don't play at all
Theodore Roosevelt

No man is justified in doing evil on the ground of expediency
Theodore Roosevelt

Far and away the best prize that life offers is the chance to work hard at work worth doing
Theodore Roosevelt

The only man who never makes a mistake is the man who never does anything
Theodore Roosevelt

I never won anything without hard labor and the exercise of my best judgment
Theodore Roosevelt

The most important single ingredient in the formula of success in knowing how to get along with people
Theodore Roosevelt

To educate a man in mind and not in morals is to educate a menace to society
Theodore Roosevelt

Patriotism means to stand by the country. It does not mean to stand by the president.
Theodore Roosevelt

We cannot do great deeds unless we're willing to do the small things that make up the sum of greatness
Theodore Roosevelt

Big jobs usually go to the men who prove their ability to outgrow small ones
Theodore Roosevelt

It is not what we have that will make us a great nation; it is the way in which we use it
    Theodore Roosevelt

Success is not counted by how high you have climbed, but by how many you brought with you
    Will Rose

A clever, imaginative, humorous request can open closed doors and closed minds
    Percy Ross

There are only 3 colors, 10 digits, and 7 notes; its what we do with them that's important
    Ruth Ross

Patience is bitter, but its fruit is sweet
    Jean-Jacques Rousseau

It does not do to dwell on dreams forget to live
    J. K. Rowling

Anything's possible if you've got enough nerve
    J.K. Rowling

I have found that if you love life, life will love you back
    Arthur Rubenstein

Hard work keeps the wrinkles out of the mind and spirit
    Helena Rubenstein

Never underestimate the power of dreams and the influence of the human spirit
    Wilma Rudolph

The potential for greatness lives within each of us
    Wilma Rudolph

When your outgo exceeds your income, your upkeep becomes your downfall
    Rick Rule

Apology is a lovely perfume; it can transform the clumsiest moment into a gracious gift
    Margaret Lee Runbeck

Happiness is not a state to arrive at, but a manner of traveling
    Margaret Lee Runbeck

One of the best ways to persuade others is with your ears - by listening to them
> *Dean Rusk*

Quality is never an accident; it is always the result of intelligent effort
> *John Ruskin*

To conquer fear is the beginning of wisdom
> *Bertrand Russell*

Happiness is not best achieved by those who seek it directly
> *Bertrand Russell*

Concentration and mental toughness are the margins of victory
> *Bill Russell*

Mediocrity is self-inflicted. Genius is self-bestowed
> *WalterRussell*

Never let the fear of striking out get in your way
> *Babe Ruth*

Yesterday's home runs don't win today's games
> *Babe Ruth*

There is a special uplifting of the spirit in the dawn chorus
> *Edward Rutherfurd*

S

Never assume the obvious is true
William Safire

Somewhere, something incredible is waiting to be known
Carl Sagan

Science is not only compatible with spirituality; it is a profound source of spirituality
Carl Sagan

Science is a way of thinking much more than it is a body of knowledge
Carl Sagan

Imagination will often carry us to worlds that never were
Carl Sagan

I intend to hold fast to my belief in the hidden strength of the human spirit
Andrei Sakharov

We must create a life worthy of ourselves
Andrei Sakharov

Failures are divided into two classes-those who thought and never did and those who did and never thought
John Salak

Intuition will tell the thinking mind where to look next
Jonas Salk

If you can drive yourself crazy, you can drive yourself happy
Karen Salmansohn

Life is like an ever changing kaleidoscope – a slight change, and all patterns alter
Sharon Salzberg

Self-reliance is the only road to true freedom
Patricia Sampson

Simplicity is the most difficult thing to secure in this world
George Sand

A child educated only at school is an uneducated child
George Santayana

The earth has music for those who listen
> *George Santayana*

Freedom is the oxygen without which science cannot breathe
> *David Sarnoff*

No matter how many goals you have achieved, you need to set a higher one
> *Jessica Savitch*

There is no substitute for paying attention
> *Diane Sawyer*

Learning to ignore things is one of the great paths to inner peace
> *Robert Sawyer*

Life is a gift of nature; but beautiful living is the gift of wisdom
> *Greek saying*

Fix the problem, not the blame
> *Japanese saying* 6-19-20

Children are our second chance to have a great parent-child relationship
> *Laura Schlessinger*

When you dare to dream, dare to follow that dream
> *Laura Schlessinger*

Find a way to say yes to things
> *Eric Schmidt*

Fast learners win
> *Eric Schmidt*

Create joy where there is no reason to do so
> *Terry Schmidt* 3-/0

Talent hits a target no one else can hit; Genius hits a target no one else can see
> *Arthur Schopenhauer*

The finest thought runs the risk of being irrevocably forgotten if we do not write it down
> *Arthur Schopenhauer*

One should use common words to say uncommon things
> *Arthur Schopenhauer*

You can wring your hands and roll up your sleeves at the same time
Pat Schroeder 6-12-20

Tough times never last, but tough people do
Robert Schuller

Build a dream and the dream will build you
Robert Schuller

Problems are not stop signs, they are guidelines
Robert Schuller 3-4

Life is like a ten-speed bicycle. Most of us have gears we never use.
Charles Schulz 2-6-20

The man who trims himself to suit everybody will soon whittle himself away
Charles Schwab

Leadership is a potent combination of strategy and character
Norman Schwarzkopf

Success is not the key to happiness. Happiness is the key to success
Albert Schweitzer

Do something wonderful, people may imitate it
Albert Schweitzer

Life isn't about how to survive the storm, but how to dance in the rain 3-22-22
Susan Lynne Schwenger

The human spirit is stronger than anything that can happen to it.
C.C. Scott

Just because you had a nightmare doesn't mean that you should stop dreaming 5-19-21
Jill Scott

Don't make the mistake of treating dogs like humans, or they'll treat you like dogs
MarthaScott

He that climbs the tall tree has won the right to the fruit
Sir Walter Scott

People who take risks are the people you'll lose against
John Sculley

129

The future belongs to those who see possibilities before they become obvious
John Sculley

Successful people are not people without problems, they are people that have learned to solve their problems
RobertSeashore

Education is when you read the fine print. Experience is what you get if you don't
Pete Seeger

Throughout my career I have been known to walk that fine line between good taste and unemployment
Lawrence Sellin

He is most powerful who has power over himself
Seneca

There is no great genius without some touch of madness
Seneca

If one does not know to which port one is sailing, no wind is favorable
Seneca

Difficulties strengthen the mind as labor strengthens the body
Seneca

Nothing happens unless first a dream
Seneca

It is a tough road that leads to the heights of greatness
Seneca

What you think of yourself is much more important than what others think of you
Seneca

Enjoy present pleasures in such a way as not to injure future ones
Seneca

The greater part of progress is the desire to progress
Seneca

Political correctness is the verbal equivalent of burning books
Gary Sepp

Be who you are and say what you feel, because those who mind don't matter and those who matter don't mind
> *Dr. Seuss*

Sometimes you will never know the value of a moment until it becomes a memory
> *Dr. Seuss*

It is better to know how to learn than to know
> *Dr. Seuss*

To the world you may be one person, to one person you may be the world
> *Dr. Seuss*

Difficulties are just things to overcome
> *Ernest Shackleton*

The world is run by the people that show up
> *William Shaefer*

It's not what you know, it's how you act on what you know
> *Scott Shafer*

Action is eloquence
> *William Shakespeare*

Our remedies oft in ourselves do lie
> *William Shakespeare*

The purest treasure mortal times afford is spotless reputation
> *William Shakespeare*

If I lose mine honor, I lose myself
> *William Shakespeare*

We know what we are, but not what we may be
> *William Shakespeare*

Love all, trust a few, do wrong to none
> *William Shakespeare*

What we need today is to secularize our religion, socialize our business, and spiritualize our politics
> *Sri Sri Ravi Shankar*

Theories crumble, but good observations never fade
> *Harlow Shapley*

"Yes" means opportunity. "No" closes doors. "Yes" kicks them wide open.
> *William Shatner*

Life isn't about finding yourself. Life is about inventing yourself.
> *George Shaw*

A ship is safe in harbor, but that is not what ships were made for
> *John Shedd*

Growth demands a temporary surrender of security
> *Gail Sheehy*

Nothing contributes so much to tranquilize the mind as a steady purpose
> *Mary Shelley*

The superior man blames himself. The inferior man blames others.
> *Don Shula*

If I fall a little bit short, I'm still further ahead than if I hadn't reached at all
> *Don Shula*

There are no shortcuts to any place worth going
> *Beverly Sills*

You may be disappointed if you fail, but you are doomed if you don't try
> *Beverly Sills*

Art is the signature of a civilization
> *Beverly Sills*

If you have integrity, nothing else matters. If you don't have integrity, nothing else matters.
> *Alan Simpson*

Education is what survives when what has been learned has been forgotten
> *B. Skinner*

A great man is the man who does something for the first time
> *Alexander Smith*

Leaders get out front and stay there by raising the standards by which they judge themselves
> *Frederick Smith*

Red meat is NOT bad for you. Now blue-green meat, THAT'S bad for you.
Tommy Smothers

Practice puts brains in your muscles
Sam Snead

An idea that's bold is worthless until sold
Don Snyder

To find yourself, think for yourself
Socrates

I cannot teach anybody anything, I can only make them think
Socrates

Love of knowledge echoes in our hearts and nourishes great thoughts
Socrates

Prefer knowledge to wealth, for the one is transitory, the other perpetual
Socrates

Leisure is the most valuable of possessions
Socrates

We cannot live better than in seeking to become better
Socrates

Wisdom begins in wonder
Socrates

No one can bar the road to truth
Aleksandr Solzhenitsyn

The line between good and evil is in the center of every human heart
AleksandrSolzhenitzyn

Always desire to learn something useful
Sophocles

I would prefer to fail with honor than win by cheating
Sophocles

No enemy is worse than bad advice
Sophocles

Fortune cannot aid those who do nothing
Sophocles

A tiger does not proclaim his tigritude, he pounces
Wole Soyinka

The minute that you make people laugh, you get them to listen
Merrie Spaeth

I dream for a living
Steven Spielberg

Trust yourself. You know more than you think you do
Benjamin Spock

When it comes to luck, you make your own
Bruce Springsteen

Fashions fade, but style is eternal
Yves St. Laurent

If I had my life to live over...I'd dare to make more mistakes next time
Nadine Stair

I am always busy, which is perhaps the chief reason why I am always well
Elizabeth Stanton

Truth is the only safe ground to stand upon
Elizabeth Stanton

Only temporary success is achieved by taking shortcuts
Roger Staubach

Scars are just another kind of memory
M.L. Stedman

The indispensable first step to getting the things you want out of life is this: decide what you want
Ben Stein

Silent gratitude isn't much use to anyone
Gertrude Stein

Ideas are like rabbits. You get a couple and learn how to handle them, and pretty soon you have a dozen
John Steinbeck

Dreaming, after all, is a form of planning
Gloria Steinem

In solitude the mind gains strength and learns to lean upon itself
Laurence Sterne

The best way to escape a problem is to solve it
Adlai Stevenson

Keep your fears to yourself, but share your courage with others
Robert Lewis Stevenson

Everyone who got where he is had to begin where he was
Robert Lewis Stevenson

Don't judge each day by the harvest you reap, but by the seeds you plant
Robert Louis Stevenson

My definition of a free society is a society where it is safe to be unpopular
Adlai Stevenson Jr.

Be careful of the friends you choose, for you will become like them
Clement Stone

Don't serve time, make time serve you
William Sutton

If your mind is empty, it is always ready for anything; it is open to everything
Shunryu Suzuki

We cannot hold a torch to light another's path without brightening our own
Ben Sweetland

The Donner Party was on track. They were not on schedule.
Bill Sweetman

All men who achieved great things have been great dreamers
Orison Swett Marden

Life is 10% what happens to you and 90% how you react to it
Charles Swindoll

Attitude is more important than the past
Charles Swindoll

The difference between something good and something great is attention to detail
> *Charles Swindoll*

A good reputation is more valuable than money
> *Publilius Syrus*

In a heated argument we are apt to lose sight of the truth
> *Publilius Syrus*

Depend not on fortune, but on conduct
> *Publilius Syrus*

You can accomplish by kindness what you cannot by force
> *Publilius Syrus*

Many receive advice, only the wise profit from it
> *Syrus*

When a person can no longer laugh at himself, it is time for others to laugh at him
> *Thomas Szasz*

T

It's always the challenge of the future, this feeling of excitement, that drives me
> *Yoshihisa Tabuchi*

Facts are many. The truth is one.
> *Rabindranath Tagore*

No labor, however humble, is dishonoring
> *The Talmud*

Leadership must be demonstrated, not announced
> *Fran Tarkenton*

They never did make them the way they used to
> *Robert Tate*

Two paradoxes are better than one; they may even suggest a solution
> *Edward Teller*

Happiness pursued eludes, happiness given returns
> *John Templeton*

The tree on the mountain takes whatever the weather brings
> *Corrie ten Boom*

If you can't feed a hundred people, then feed just one
> *Mother Teresa*

Kind words can be short and easy to speak, but their echoes are truly endless
> *Mother Teresa*

We shall never know all the good a simple smile can do
> *Mother Teresa*

Be alone, that is when ideas are born
> *Nikola Tesla*

A good laugh is sunshine in the house
> *William Thackeray*

The problem with socialism is that you eventually run out of other people's money
> *Margaret Thatcher*

You may have to fight a battle more than once to win it
> *Margaret Thatcher*

137

Europe was created by history. America was created by philosophy.
    Margaret Thatcher

I praise loudly. I blame softly.
    Catherine the Great

I'm never gonna stop the rain by complaining
    B.J. Thomas

Sometimes the best helping hand you can get is a good, firm push
    JoAnn Thomas

Do a little more each day than you think you possibly can
    Lowell Thomas 3-31-21

Be true to your work, your word, and your friend
    HenryDavid Thoreau

Men are born to succeed, not fail
    Henry David Thoreau

It is never too late to give up your prejudices
    Henry David Thoreau

Live the life you've always imagined
    HenryDavid Thoreau

Many men go fishing their entire lives without knowing it is not fish they are after
    HenryDavid Thoreau

Be not simply good; be good for something
    HenryDavid Thoreau

That man is richest whose pleasures are the cheapest.
    Henry David Thoreau

It's not what you look at that matters, it's what you see
    Henry David Thoreau 5-20-20

It is not enough to be industrious; so are the ants
    Henry David Thoreau

The universe is wider than our views of it
    Henry David Thoreau

The secret of happiness is freedom, and the secret of freedom, courage
    Thucydides

It is better to know some of the questions than all of the answers
James Thurber

Follow the grain in your own wood
Howard Thurman

Traditions are group efforts to keep the unexpected from happening
Barbara Tober

Knowledge is the most democratic source of power
Alvin Toffler

Little by little, one can travel far
JRR Tolkien

It's the job that's never started that takes the longest to finish
JRR. Tolkien

Not all who wander are lost
JRR. Tolkien

The two most powerful warriors are patience and time
Leo Tolstoy

Nobody gets successful by being lazy
Bruno Tonioli

True leadership must be for the benefit of the followers, not the enrichment of the leaders
Robert Townsend

Luck is what happens when preparedness meets opportunity
Brian Tracy

The more you seek security, the less of it you have
Brian Tracy

If you want to make others happy, start by living the kind of life and doing the kinds of things that make you happy
Brian Tracy

An ordinary person with a well thought out plan will run circles around a genius without one
Brian Tracy

The future belongs to the risk takers, not the security seekers
Brian Tracy

Worry is a form of negative goal setting
> *Brian Tracy*

You develop courage by behaving courageously any time courage is called for
> *Brian Tracy*

Develop an attitude of gratitude, and give thanks for everything that happens to you
> *Brian Tracy*

Successful people are simply those with success habits
> *Brian Tracy*

The more credit you give away, the more will come back to you
> *Brian Tracy*

If you want more luck, take more chances. Be more active.
> *Brian Tracy*

Never say anything about yourself you do not want to come true
> *Brian Tracy*

Goals allow you to control the direction of change in your favor
> *Brian Tracy*

All successful people are big dreamers
> *Brian Tracy*

Your past is not your potential
> *Brian Tracy*

Amateurs train until they get it right, professionals train until they can't get it wrong
> *Training truism*

All leaders are readers
> *Harry Truman*

It is amazing what you can accomplish if you do not care who gets the credit
> *Harry Truman*

To be able to lead others, a man must be willing to go forward alone
> *Harry Truman*

Inreading the lives of great men, the first victory that they won was over themselves
> *Harry Truman*

We must have strong minds, ready to accept facts as they are
Harry Truman

The reward of suffering is experience
Harry Truman

How far would Moses have gone if he had taken a poll in Egypt?
HarryTruman

Courage usually involves a highly realistic estimate of the odds that must be faced
Margaret Truman

Sometimes your best investments are the ones you don't make
Donald Trump

If you're going to be thinking, you may as well think big
Donald Trump

Every great dream begins with a dreamer
Harriet Tubman

To enjoy the glow of good health, you must exercise
Gene Tunney

A man should never be a judge of his father
Ovan Turgenev

Forgiveness is an absolute necessity for continued human existence
Desmond Tutu

Always do right. This will gratify some people and astonish the rest
Mark Twain

Action speaks louder than words but not nearly as often
Mark Twain

The best way to cheer yourself up is to try to cheer somebody else up
Mark Twain

I can live for months on a good complement
Mark Twain

Courage is resistance to fear, mastery of fear, not absence of fear
Mark Twain

Whenever you find yourself on the side of the majority, it's time to pause and reflect
Mark Twain

Sail away from the safe harbor. Explore. Dream. Discover
> *Mark Twain*

Twenty years from now you will be more disappointed by the things that you didn't do than by the ones that you did do
> *Mark Twain*

You can't depend on your eyes when your imagination is out of focus
> *Mark Twain*

The secret of getting ahead is getting started
> *Mark Twain*

Professionalism is knowing how to do it, when to do it, and doing it
> *FrankTyger*

He who knows others is wise. He who knows himself is enlightened.
> *Lao Tzu*

Mastering yourself is true power
> *Lao Tzu*

When I let go of what I am, I become what I might be
> *Lao Tzu* 9-17-20

Opportunities multiply as they are seized
> *Sun Tzu*

The leader of any group is the one who learns from the wisdom of all involved
> *Sun Tzu*

V

You can't run in place or someone will pass you by
Jim Valvano

If you want your children to keep their feet on the ground, put some responsibility on their shoulders
Abigail Van Buren

If you want your place in the sun, you've got to put up with a few blisters
Abigail Van Buren

Some people are so afraid to die that they never begin to live
Henry Van Dyke

If you truly love Nature, you will find beauty everywhere
Vincent Van Gogh

I dream my paintings and then I paint my dream
Vincent van Gogh

It is less important to redistribute wealth than to redistribute opportunity
Arthur Vandenberg

You only get one life, so you might as well make it a happy one
Nia Vardalos

Great thoughts always come from the heart
Marquis De Vauvenargues

I try not to break the rules, but merely to test their elasticity
Bill Veeck

Science is made up of mistakes, but they lead little by little to the truth
Jules Verne

Love truth, and pardon error
Voltaire

Judge a man by his questions, not his answers
Voltaire

A witty saying proves nothing
Voltaire

I have learned to use the word impossible with the greatest caution.
Wernher von Braun

Mountains cannot be surmounted except by winding paths.
> *Johann Von Goethe*

Knowing is not enough; we must apply. Willing is not enough; we must do
> *JohannVon Goethe*

Treat people as if they were what they ought to be
> *JohannVon Goethe*

Who dares nothing, need hope for nothing
> *Johann Von Schiller*

To acquire knowledge, one must study; but to acquire wisdom, one must observe
> *Marilyn vos Savant*

W

Joy is not in things; it is in us
Richard Wagner

There is no life without humor
Rufus Wainwright

The results you achieve will be in direct proportion to the effort you apply
Denis Waitley

Belief is the ignition switch that gets you off the launching pad
Denis Waitley

It makes little difference what's happening out there. It's how you take it that counts
DenisWaitley

Chase your passion, not your pension
Dennis Waitley

Losers make promises they often break. Winners make commitments they always keep.
Dennis Waitley

Words are plentiful, but deeds are precious
Lech Walesa

The most common way people give up their power is by thinking they don't have any
Alice Walker

When you look up, you go up
Herschel Walker

Friends and good manners will carry you where money won't go
Margaret Walker

Every man dies. Not every man really lives
WilliamWallace

People who cannot find time for recreation are obliged sooner or later to find time for illness
John Wanamaker

Courtesy is the one coin you can never have too much of or be stingy with
John Wanamaker

Success is more a function of consistent common sense than it is of genius
    An Wang

Team members need ultra clear priorities in order to work fast
    Steve Ward

The pessimist borrows trouble; the optimist lends encouragement
    William Ward

If you can imagine it you can create it. If you can dream it, you can become it
    William Ward

Curiosity is the wick in the candle of learning
    William Ward

Real optimism is aware of problems but recognizes the solutions
    William Ward

Adversity causes some men to break, others to break records
    William Ward

A cloudy day is no match for a sunny disposition. 5-20-22
    William Ward

When we seek to discover the best in others, we somehow bring out the best in ourselves 7-24-22
    WilliamWard

Thorough preparation is its own luck
    Howard Wasdin

There are two ways of exerting one's strength: one is pushing down, the other is pulling up
    Booker T. Washington

If you want to lift yourself up, lift up someone else
    Booker T.Washington 2-20

An inch of progress is worth more than a yard of complaint
    Booker T.Washington

It's wonderful what we can do if we're always doing
    George Washington

To err is nature, to rectify error is glory
    George Washington

The greatest part of our happiness depends on our dispositions, not our circumstances
Martha Washington

A manager is an assistant to his men
Thomas Watson Sr.

School is a building which has fours walls with tomorrow inside
LonWatters

Letting your mind play is the best way to solve problems
Bill Watterson

The only safe ship in a storm is leadership
Faye Wattleton

To get what you want, STOP doing what isn't working
Dennis Weaver

Events don't cause stress. Thoughts do.
HendrieWeisinger 9-1-20

Willingness to change is a strength
Jack Welch

Change before you have to
Jack Welch

Face reality as it is, not as it was or as you wish it to be
Jack Welch

You can't fake listening. It shows.
Raquel Welch

Details create the big picture
Sandy Wells

When people see that their ideas count, their dignity is raised
Jack Welsh

A man's health can be judged by which he takes two at a time -- pills or stairs
Joan Welsh

You are never too old to become younger
Mae West

You only live once, but if your do it right, once is enough
Mae West

Before a war military science seems a real science, like astronomy; but after a war it seems more like astrology
    Rebecca West

If only we'd stop trying to be happy we'd have a pretty good time
    Edith Wharton

Time is nature's way of keeping everything from happening all at once
    John Wheeler

Genius is more often found in a cracked pot than a whole one
    E. B. White

Children are the living messages we send to a time we will not see
    John Whitehead

The future is no more uncertain than the present
    Walt Whitman

Action makes more fortune than caution
    Charlotte Whitton

Peace is our gift to each other
    Elie Wiesel

Everyone is born a king, and most people die in exile
    Oscar Wilde

The pursuit of perfection often impedes improvement
    George Will

I would not waste my life in friction when it could be turned into momentum
    Frances Willard

I believe I can adapt to anything
    Deron Williams

A lifetime is not nearly enough time to learn music
    John Williams

Enthusiasm is the most important thing in life
    Tennessee Williams

The practice of forgiveness is our most important contribution to the healing of the world
    Marianne Williamson

The whisper of temptation can be heard farther than the loudest call to duty
> *Early Wilson*

The ear of the leader must ring with the voices of the people
> *Woodrow Wilson*

A friend is someone who walks in when others walk out
> *Walter Winchell*

An optimist is someone who gets treed by a lion but enjoys the scenery
> *Walter Winchell*

The more you celebrate life, the more there is to celebrate
> *Oprah Winfrey*

Turn your wounds into wisdom
> *Oprah Winfrey*

Create the highest, grandest vision possible for your life, because you become what you believe
> *Oprah Winfrey*

The greatest lesson of life is that your are responsible for your life
> *Oprah Winfrey*

Take from every experience what it has to offer you
> *Oprah Winfrey*

The biggest adventure you can ever take is to live the life of your dreams
> *Oprah Winfrey*

Where there is no struggle, there is no strength
> *Oprah Winfrey*

Assumptions are the termites of relationships
> *HenryWinkler*

Doubt grows with knowledge
> *Johann Wolfgang von Goethe*

A dog lover can only love his dog; a dog trainer can love and train.
> *Richard Wolters*

You cannot live a perfect day without doing something for someone who will never be able to repay you
> *John Wooden*

Never mistake activity for achievement
    John Wooden

Nothing will work unless you do
    John Wooden

Respect a man and he will do all the more
    John Wooden

Do not let what you cannot do interfere with what you can do
    John Wooden

Do not let what you cannot do interfere with what you can do
    John Wooden

Ability may get you to the top, but it takes character to keep you there
    John Wooters

To steal ideas from one person is plagiarism; to steal from many is research
    Steven Wright

When two men in business always agree, one of them is unnecessary
    William Wrigley Jr.

Y

The excitement of learning separates youth from old age
 Rosalyn Yalow

As long as you're learning you're not old
 Rosalyn Yalow

Education is not the filling of a pail, but the lighting of a fire
 William Yeats

Z

Worry is a misuse of the imagination
Dan Zadra

Never underestimate the power of apology
Ron Zemke

Happiness is the absence of the striving for happiness
Zhuangzi

A goal without a plan is just a wish
Zig Ziglar

Those without goals are destined to work for those with goals
Zig Ziglar

A big goal is just several little goals in a row
Zig Ziglar

If you don't think everyday is a great day, try going without one
Zig Ziglar

Your attitude, not your aptitude, will determine your altitude
Zig Ziglar

People often say that motivation doesn't last. Well, neither does bathing -- that's why we recommend it daily
Zig Ziglar

Building a better you is the first step to building a better America
Zig Ziglar

A goal properly set is halfway reached
Zig Ziglar

Every choice you make has an end result
Zig Ziglar

An optimist is someone who goes after Moby Dick in a rowboat and takes the tartar sauce with him
Zig Ziglar

Efficiency is doing things right. Effectiveness is doing the right thing
Zig Ziglar

The most beautiful philosophy in the world won't work if you don't
Zig Ziglar

Failure takes the path of least persistence
> *Zig Ziglar*

We should autograph our work with excellence
> *Zig Ziglar*

Every job is a self portrait of the person that did it
> *Zig Ziglar*

You cannot consistently perform in a manner which is inconsistent with the way you see yourself
> *Zig Ziglar*

Positive thinking will let you do everything better than negative thinking will
> *Zig Ziglar*

There is a difference between standard of living and quality of life
> *ZigZiglar*

The artist is nothing without the gift, but the gift is nothing without the work
> *Emile Zola*

Made in the USA
Monee, IL
08 February 2020